The Synoptic Gospels

Bible Studies
for the
Contemporary Church

The Synoptic Gospels

Bible Studies
for the
Contemporary Church

John F. Johnson

Whole Person Associates
Duluth, Minnesota

Whole Person Associates
210 W. Michigan
Duluth, MN 55802–1908

800-247-6789

The Synoptic Gospels: Bible Studies for the Contemporary Church

Printed in the United States of America

ISBN 978-1-57025-248-3

Library of Congress Control Number: 2006921366

Contents

Jesus the Messiah
Witness of the Gospel According to Matthew

The Christian Faith
According to the Gospel of Mark

Witness to Ministry
According to the Gospel of Luke

Preface

Toward the close of the first Christian century Clement of Rome asserts that the apostles received from Christ the good news that he died for our sins and was raised for our forgiveness. Fully assured by the resurrection, the apostles went forth proclaiming the word of God with confidence (Epistle to the Corinthians, xliii. c. A.D. 95). They and other disciples, both men and women, were to witness that which they had experienced. They were persuaded by the Holy Spirit that their joyous message was to be shared with the entire world (Acts 1:8; 2:32).

Their witness at first assumes the form of verbal proclamation. In the course of time it was only natural that it should assume written form as well. Papias of Hierapolis (A.D. 130) maintains that he learned and recorded the truth from those whom he designates elders, by which he evidently means apostles since he names them. One of the traditions he cites informs us that Mark became an assistant to Peter and the interpreter of his teachings. Mark wrote an accurate, if not completely orderly, account of as much as he could recall of the words and deeds of Christ. Some modern commentators are convinced that Mark became an early member of the Christian community. He was thus privy to information quite apart from his close association with Peter. According to Papias, Matthew recorded in the Hebrew (or Aramaic) tongue certain logia, i.e., sayings of the Lord. These logia, most likely oracular utterances similar to those attributed to Old Testament prophets, would constitute an eyewitness account of Jesus' teachings. Each reader, comments Papias, interpreted or translated these logia to the best of his ability.

Some twenty years later another Christian writer, Justin Martyr, writes that the baptized assemble together on the day known as the "day of the sun" for prayer and thanksgiving. The Eucharist is celebrated and the "Memoirs of the Apostles," called Gospels, are read (Apology I, lxvi-lxvii. c. A.D. 150). Toward the close of that century, Irenaeus of

Lyons undertook a vigorous defense of Christian teaching against various heretical sectarians. He asserts that Matthew published his Gospel in his own tongue among Hebrews while Peter and Paul were preaching in Rome. A number of modern scholars argue with considerable cogency that Matthew actually wrote a source document in Aramaic, known as Q, from the German word *Quelle* (source). This became the basis of the Gospels, which eventually came to be known as Matthew and Luke. Irenaeus also declares that Mark recorded Peter's preaching while Luke composed the work containing the teaching of his mentor, Paul. The same writer further remarks that John produced a Gospel while residing in Ephesus. A work known as *Muratorian Fragment*, written at approximately the same time, attributes the third Gospel to Luke, the physician whom Paul chose as his traveling companion. Though not an eyewitness, Luke could trace the events of the Lord's life as he was able to ascertain them, beginning with the birth of John (the Baptizer). The fourth Gospel Irenaeus attributes to John, who narrated in his own name all that he and Andrew were able to recall.

According to this rather early tradition, then, the Gospels are to be considered written apostolic witness to the ministry of Jesus. The Gospels, testifies Irenaeus, provide God's plan of redemptive salvation. Other Church Fathers reecho that conviction. The books were written solely for the purpose of proclaiming the message, which Christ committed to the whole church. Since the ultimate goal of all Christian witness is to lead hearers to a living faith in Jesus Christ as Lord and Savior, the purpose of the Gospels may be defined as engendering the response of faith to the good news of salvation.

The importance of the Gospels as genuinely authoritative apostolic witness to Jesus is clearly discerned from a phenomenon, which arose early in the life of the church. Spurious, untrustworthy, highly imaginative, and even heretical "Gospels" proliferated under the names of apostles. They sought to clothe with apostolic authority bizarre, fanciful, cultic and totally false teachings, which were being fostered by a number of rival movements. They claim to provide details of messianic teachings otherwise unknown. They freely invent incidents and devise situations to bolster their own theological peculiarities. Indeed, Origen (c. A.D. 200) can exclaim that the church has only four Gospels. Heretical movements boast of many!

Of the four Gospels, three have been recognized by scholars and non-scholars alike as being very closely related in delineating the mind, mission and ministry of Jesus. For that reason they are called Synoptic Gospels, i.e., able to be seen together. This is an appropriate observation. A close comparison of texts and order reveals a common, though certainly not always uniform, approach. All report that Jesus undertakes his mission after that of John the Baptizer is terminated. All narrate Jesus' baptism, trials and testing by Satan and assorted responses to his message. Locale of his activity is chiefly Galilee, although segments of the narrative appear to be more topical in nature than chronological or topographical. There is at least one Passover observance. Apostles and disciples are summoned to follow him. There is extended controversy and polemic against Jewish legalism. Jesus is involved with scribes, elders, Pharisees and Sadducees.

The Synoptics all incorporate into the record the momentous and dramatic confession of Jesus as Messiah on the part of his disciples. All locate the incident in Caesarea Philippi. All report the event of transfiguration. They further include instruction on the part of Jesus as to the meaning of true discipleship, life in the kingdom of God, and confrontations leading to this crucifixion. Each witnesses his resurrection. Each also relates parables and aphorisms, though not all are found in any one Gospel. Some of the events, mighty acts, saying and teaching of our Lord thus enjoy a double, even triple, attestation. At the time each Gospel has its own distinctive style, approach, outline and purpose.

The Synoptics are, by tradition, attributed to Matthew, Mark and Luke. Interestingly enough, only Matthew bears the name of an apostle. However, Mark and Luke are deemed bearers of the apostolic teaching of Peter and Paul. Origen simply remarks that the first Gospel was written by Matthew, tax collector turned apostle, for converts from Judaism. Mark composed his work following the instruction of Peter. Luke brought the preaching of Paul to Gentile converts. Most commentators still hold that Mark is the primary source of the life and ministry of the Lord.

A good deal of scholarship known as biblical criticism has been applied to the Gospels. Such criticism analyzes and evaluates facets of the record such as historical accuracy, use of the sayings of Jesus, the framework in which the narratives appear, various literary forms found in the collections of materials available to the writers, revisions and additions by the penmen, relationship between parallel accounts of the same incidents, etc. Such research is often negative and destructive. But much of it has enriched and continues to enrich our knowledge and understanding of the nature of the Gospels and their proper place in the life of the church.

The Synoptics make no claim to be exact or complete biographical accounts of Jesus' activity, at least in our contemporary understanding of the term. Neither do they claim to be simple historical literature, which follows strict criteria of historiography. True, Luke displays considerable interest in chronological data. He explicitly states that his sources are guaranteed by eyewitnesses and servants of the Word. But he does not claim that his record is in any way exhaustive. Indeed, the author specifically says of the fourth Gospel that it is not a complete account (John 20:30; 21:25). Therefore we do not uncritically approach the Synoptics (or John) as mere biographical record or simple historical narrative. They draw a portrait, which provides an authentic and authoritative witness to the ministry of Jesus. They put us in touch with apostolic proclamation, the teachings of the early church and the faith confessed by the early Christian community out of which the Gospels evolved. As has been aptly put forth by many, they reliably transmit the truth.

Having withstood the test of usage and time, Matthew, Mark and Luke commend themselves to us today. They are reliable witnesses to that extraordinary ministry of Jesus Christ through which God summons to repentance, faith and new life in that kingdom which shall have no end.

Procedural Note

In order to gain maximum benefit from this study, it is suggested that you read each Gospel under consideration. If doing so in one sitting is not feasible, cover it in two or three sittings, following outlines presented. While any number of helpful outlines are readily available, those presented in this study attempt to capture the depiction of Jesus' messianic message and ministry as acts and scenes of a divine drama.

It is important to realize that chapters and verses (as well as titles) of the Gospels are not part of original manuscripts. They were devised in the interest of easy and simple reference. Chapter divisions are found in copies that go back to the thirteenth century. The addition of verses can be traced to the middle of the sixteenth century.

A reading of each Gospel in a version with which you are comfortable and familiar is also highly recommended. Then, perhaps, reread the Gospel in a different version. As you begin this study, read the biblical text covered by each chapter of the study. After reading the material provided by this study, you may want to reread the text of the Gospel which has been treated. If you are part of a class, the instructor may have additional suggestions. The real purpose of any outline or study is to lead the reader into the Scriptures, which testify powerfully to the saving grace of God in Jesus Christ. As you begin each section, pray the Holy Spirit to give you ears to hear the good news and eyes to see in Jesus your Savior and Lord.

Problems dealing with date, place of composition, use of sources, and relationship to other Gospels are important and fascinating. But we consign them to experts to carry out a careful investigation of all such things. Furthermore, no attempt has been made to suggest or consult parallel passages found in other Gospels. Most versions of the Bible provide handy cross-references. One may with profit examine them. But the basic text of the study is the individual Gospel at hand. For that reason also, references to other biblical books have been kept to a bare minimum.

Jesus the Messiah

Witness of the Gospel
According to Matthew

Introduction

This study will assist the reader in understanding the witness to the Christian Faith made by the Gospel According to Matthew and in realizing how deeply that witness is rooted in the teachings, traditions and motifs of the Old Testament. References to other books of the New Testament are limited; echoes, citations, references and allusions from the Old Testament are numerous. While intended to be non-technical in its approach, problems in textual, literary and historical criticism have not been ignored. Its primary aim is not to introduce the uncritical reader to problems with which trained theologians and scholars wrestle, but to enrich the reader with background sufficient for a renewed appreciation for the powerful testimony to Jesus the Messiah, which this Gospel affords.

Roots of the Christian community lie deeply embedded in the community of Israel. The old covenant found form and substance in the promises, which God established with Abraham, Isaac and Jacob so many centuries before the life, death and exaltation of Jesus the Messiah, the Son of the live God (16:16). For in raising Jesus from the dead, God revealed not only his own glory, power and faithfulness, God designated Jesus both Lord and Messiah. So the Christian Faith is a historical faith. It centers in a life lived out on the plain of human history in a series of remembered and recited events. It is linked to words of promise spoken by Yahweh within the continuum of human experience embodied uniquely and decisively in Jesus. The good news of all that God has done (and does) in Christ's death and resurrection is known as gospel.

The remembered and recited events of Jesus' life and works, suffering and death, resurrection and exaltation, had to be more than mere oral reminiscences of a religious tradition. The story was committed to writing. Later it came to be known as the Gospel. While early Christians knew of only one Gospel, by the year 150 "Memoirs" of the apostles were referred to as Gospels. As the incipient canon of the New

Testament developed a four-fold Gospel, it came to be recognized as an authentic account of Jesus' life and ministry according to Matthew, Mark, Luke and John. This occurred even though none of the accounts calls itself a Gospel or even identifies its author. By the year 250, the tradition was apparently so well established that the four Gospels as we know them were "alone undisputed in the Church."

In the traditional order of New Testament writings the first Gospel is attributed to Matthew. While certain sayings, or logia of Jesus, were said to have been compiled by Matthew, Origen (c. A.D. 200) comments that the first Gospel was written by Matthew, an apostle of Jesus Christ. It is published "in their language" (Hebrew or Aramaic) for Jewish converts. There is no certain evidence that this Gospel, at least as we know it, came from his pen. The author most likely used the Gospel of Mark as a resource work, along with various narratives and parables, which enjoyed wide circulation among Jewish Christians.

The Gospel bearing Matthew's name seems to have originated in Antioch of Syria where Christians were quite numerous. It presupposes considerable acquaintance with Old Testament events, teachings, and traditions. Its first readers must have been as Jewish as its author and the book was undoubtedly used for missionary purposes as well as for instructional new converts. Matthew freely entitles Jesus as the Messiah (fourteen times) and accords him such related messianic titles as Son of David, Emmanuel and King (seventeen times). Jesus is confessed as both Son of God (nine times) and Son of Man (thirty times), reminiscent of the apocalyptic vision of Daniel. He is born Savior of the world. He is presented as preacher and interpreter of Torah (5:17–7:27). He clothes his apostles with prophetic authority as he commissions them to make disciples of all the nations by baptizing and teaching in the name of Father, Son and Holy Spirit.

Many narratives recounted by Matthew appear in Mark in considerably condensed form. This has given rise to the conviction that Matthew is much more concerned with the teaching authority of Jesus than with bare history. Some who study this Gospel discover in it an "architectonic grandeur." They are able to identify seven so-called great discourses of Jesus as well as ten great themes of his teaching. All relate to the kingdom of God inaugurated with his life, death and resurrection. Specific references to the Old Testament (five in the first two chapters, more than one hundred and sixty in the entire book) presume not only a Jewish audience; they bespeak an unquestioned desire to demonstrate that events of Jesus' life and ministry fulfill salvation promises made by Yahweh (Cf. 1:22; 2:15). But fulfillment means more than mere correspondence of events with prediction; it means filling reality with ultimate meaning (3:15). Jesus did not come to abolish the Law and Prophets, but rather to fulfill them (5:17). This fact provides ultimate significance for the community of God's redeemed people.

Dating of the Gospel cannot be ascertained with any kind of irrefutable precision. Most likely, the date lies in the early 80's. The destruction of Jerusalem occurred in A.D. 70. After this catastrophe, the sect of Pharisees, whose unbending legalism Jesus often challenged, sought to preserve Judaism against both Roman paganism and a growing Christian movement. By the time this Gospel was composed and circulated, Pharisaic Judaism had gained ascendancy and represented orthodox beliefs. Often linked with the scribes and elders, the sect of Pharisees claimed to find both their authority and authenticity in Mosaic Law. Matthew stresses the unbridgeable opposition, which existed between Pharisaic Judaism and Messianic Christianity. Jesus is greater than Moses, greater than the Temple, greater than Torah. His authority derives from the fact that he is Son of God and Messiah, attested by his resurrection from the dead. In him the promised kingdom of God has arrived (4:17). Matthew expresses the response and reaction of those who had been affected by Messiah's ministry:

The crowds were astonished, for he taught with authority (7:28).

You are the Messiah, the Son of the living God (16:16).

They came and worshipped him (28:9).

A fourth-century church historian cites the opinion of earlier writers who claim that the Gospel according to Matthew deserves to be placed first in any listing or order. Reasons for such an opinion may be obscure. They may even reflect a good bit of theological bias. But this Gospel does continue to demand high regard as a witness to the ministry of the Messiah and to the beliefs of the Christian community. For one thing, Matthew presents itself as a comprehensive Gospel. It incorporates into the narrative of the life of Jesus the most detailed record of his birth, life, teachings, death resurrection and commission to his disciples. All of these elements are combined into a ready hand-book, which served to instruct members of the community and those still without.

Matthew can speak convincingly to Jewish readers who might be pon-dering or contemplating a confession of the messiahship of Jesus. It not only accurately describes their customs and beliefs; at the same time it witnesses so clearly to Jesus of Nazareth as the true consolation of Israel and ultimate fulfiller of its hopes.

Matthew has often been characterized as the churchly Gospel. Not only does it employ the word "church" (16:18; 18:17), it bestows upon the fellowship of faith the power, presence and promise of its Lord while it awaits the parousia of the ascended and glorified Messiah.

The closing chapters of this Gospel have been highlighted as an ex-quisite literary work. The One who is proclaimed royal Son of David (21:9; 15) and hailed as the One, who comes in the name of the Lord, faces his impending passion with rare royal dignity. Amid capture and trial, betrayal and denial, intense spiritual struggles and physical degra-dation, cruel crucifixion and death, Jesus displays a quiet, but nonethe-less, eloquent royal bearing. He knows that legions of angels are his for the asking (26:53). He knows that the very enemies before whom he is standing and being judged will behold the majestic glory of the Son of Man coming in power (26:64). Matthew alone records that at Jesus' death tombs, symbols of death and defeat, are unsealed by the shak-ing of the very earth of which they are a part (27:52). The final scene sketched by this Gospel depicts the resurrected Lord, King of all kings and Lord of all lords, assuring his disciples that all power in heaven and on earth is his (28:18).

The Gospel lends itself to several outlines. The one chosen here is sim-ple. But it emphasizes the witness, which Matthew gives to Jesus as Messiah and Lord.

Part One

Prologue and Ministry
of the Messiah

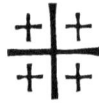

╬╬

CHAPTER ONE

Beginnings of the Gospel of Jesus the Messiah
Matthew 1 & 2

The book of the genealogy of Jesus Christ, the Son of David, the Son of Abraham, introduces more than a mere historical recitation of a family tree. It suggests a process, a creative movement in human history. Promise has received fulfillment. The title, Christ (Hebrew: Messiah, anointed), defines the mission and ministry of Jesus through whom God has inaugurated the new age (4:17). The genealogy attests that Jesus, born of Joseph's wife, Mary, is the goal of divine history. When early Christians confessed Jesus to be Messiah, they claimed participation in the covenant community, the people of God who live by faith in the promises made to Abraham (8:11).

Genealogy of Jesus the Messiah (1:1–17)
In tracing the genealogy, Matthew reveals his predilection for numbers, which he may have deliberately employed as teaching aids. Three and seven are most popular. He distinguishes three divisions in the genealogical record (1:17) and describes three temptations, which inaugurate Jesus' public ministry (4:1–11). There are three miracles of healing (8:1–15), three miracles of power (8:23–9:8), three miracles of restoration (9:18–34), three prayers in Gethsemane (26:39–44) and three denials by Peter (26:69–75). The writer makes use of the number seven in a similar manner. Seven mountains serve as scenes for important events. Seven petitions comprise the Lord's Prayer (6:9–13). There are seven evil spirits (12:45), seven loaves (15:34), seven brothers (22:25) and seven references to the thirty pieces of silver (27:3–10). Moreover, Peter is directed to forgive seven times seventy times (18:22). In Hebrew thought the number three is holy, while seven symbolizes perfection.

Matthew arranges the genealogy in three sections of fourteen names.

It is fascinating to some that the Hebrew letters of the name David have the numerical value of fourteen. The genealogy establishes legal descent from the royal line. The term, Son of Abraham, though not as widely known or used as Son of David, links Jesus with the promise established with the patriarch (Genesis 12). For Matthew, the genealogy reveals that divinely guided historical process by which Jesus enters human history.

Birth of Jesus the Messiah (1:18–25)

The birth is described as both spiritual and virginal conception. Jewish law declared engagement as tantamount to marriage. Before the consummation of their marriage, Mary is found pregnant. Two courses of action, both distasteful to Joseph, are open to him. He can publicly dismiss Mary and thus dissolve the relationship. Or he can charge Mary with adultery. If condemned, she would be stoned to death. Joseph chooses to divorce Mary quietly, thus sparing her public condemnation.

Joseph is led to understand the creative role of the Holy Spirit in the conception (1:20–21). The extraordinary announcement has a parallel in Genesis 18:1–15. The Holy Spirit creates new life as the presence of God in his community. Reference to Isaiah 7:14 underlines the firm conviction that in the person of Jesus, God has come to his people. Jesus is Immanu-El, i.e., God is with us. The name, Joshua (Greek: Jesus), means salvation. Deliverance and salvation are a reality whenever God is present with his people in a unique revelation of his grace. After Pentecost, the apostolic witness centered in the grand truth that God raised and exalted Jesus as Savior to give repentance and forgiveness of sins to Israel (Acts 5:30–32).

Light for Revelation to Gentile Nations 2:1–23

The Messiah fulfills Israel's hopes because he fulfills Israel's prophecies. In this section of his Gospel, Matthew records four such instances, which bear decisive testimony to Jesus' role and mission. We see that 2:6 quotes Micah 5:1 and II Samuel 5:2; 2:15 refers to Hosea 11:1; 2:18 cites Jeremiah 31:15; 2:23 is quite likely at least an allusion to Isaiah 11:1 or 49:6.

As the true glory of Israel, the one to whom Moses points in predictive prophecy (Deuteronomy 18:15), Jesus is greater than Moses. Nonetheless, Christian, Jewish-Christian and Jewish readers alike must realize the striking similarities between Jesus and Moses. Moses is persecuted by Pharaoh (Exodus 1:15–22) – Jesus is persecuted by Herod. Pharaoh massacres male infants in Egypt (Exodus 1:1ff) – Herod massacres infants in Bethlehem. Pharaoh forces Moses to flee into exile to Midian (Exodus 1:11–15) – Herod forces Jesus to flee into exile in Egypt. Moses returns to Egypt following the death of Pharaoh (Exodus 4:19) – Jesus returns to Palestine after the death of Herod. Moses spends forty days and nights fasting in the desert (Exodus 24:18) – Jesus spends forty days and nights fasting in the desert.

The place of the Messiah's birth is Bethlehem, the ancient city of David, second king of Israel. Herod, grossly misnamed the Great, was more Edomite than Hebrew. He must be distinguished from Herod Antipas, before whom Jesus appeared some thirty years later. Herod was appointed king of Judah in 40 B.C. by the Roman Senate. According to modern chronological reckoning, he died 4 B.C.. The same reckoning stipulates the birth of Jesus as 6 or 7 B.C.. Herod was an utterly corrupt, despotic and self-serving ruler from whose excessive cruelties not even his own family was exempted. To curry favor with the people he launched an ambitious public works program, which included rebuilding of the Temple (begun c. 20 B.C.). One of the spurious charges leveled against Jesus was that Jesus claimed to be able to destroy that Temple and rebuild it in only three days (26:61).

The notion of a universal king hailing from the East had gained wide currency in the ancient world. A single star, or conjunction of planets, such as Jupiter or Saturn, serves as a sign that his kind had appeared in Judah. Magi, originally a priestly class of scholars of Persia, were noted astronomers and mathematicians. The guiding star recalls the pillar that led Israel through the wilderness (Exodus 13:21). The Testament of Levi, an apocryphal work, declares that the star of the Messiah will arise in the heavens (18:3). The Messiah himself is referred to as a star in Numbers 24:17. As the Magi fall down in worship before him, they herald the Messiah as the light of divine revelation to Gentile nations. Later Christians saw this incident as reflecting Psalm 72:11 and Isaiah 60:1–6. Gifts offered by the Magi have often been viewed as signs and symbols of Jesus' royalty, divinity and death.

Discussion

1. What is Matthew's purpose in citing the Old Testament so frequently?

2. What principle of biblical interpretation is emphasized by this Gospel?

3. How essential to the Christology of the New Testament is virginal conception?

CHAPTER TWO

Beginnings of the Ministry of the Messiah Matthew 3 & 4

Nearly three decades in the life of Jesus pass without comment or reference by Matthew. Luke refers to the visit of the twelve-year-old Jesus in Jerusalem at a Feast of Passover. He reports simply that the child increased in wisdom, stature, in favor with God and in favor with man (Luke 2:41–52). Regarding the so-called silent years that follow, unreliable stories and fanciful illusions abound in apocryphal sources. None of the canonical Gospels clothe them with reliability or significance.

Ministry of John the Baptizer 3:1–12

The Gospel according to Luke recounts the annunciation and birth of John. Famed Jewish historian, Josephus (Antiquities), provides a non-biblical witness to the brief ministry of John. He preached a message of repentance, administered a baptism, gathered disciples and was executed by Herod Antipas. The puppet king, who depended on Roman approval to maintain his position, feared that the wilderness prophet would foment spiritual or political rebellion. Both would seriously jeopardize Herod's claim to rule.

Though none of the Gospels affirm it, John may have been a member of the monastic type Hebrew sect known as Essenes. It attracted followers of a more meditative bent than the scholarly Pharisees, priestly Sadducees and revolutionary Zealots. John may have even have been an adherent of the Qumran community, which was located in the wilderness area near the Dead Sea. The Essenes practiced a purification rite, proclaimed repentance for remission of sins and expected a dramatic eschatological movement of cosmic proportions. It would usher in the messianic age and establish the rule (kingdom) of God on earth.

Pious Jews avoided the name, Yahweh, substituting in its place the names, Adonai or Elohim. Similarly, devout Jews often substituted the word, heaven(s), for God. John's rite prepared the way for the Messiah's ministry. Matthew interprets that ministry as a sign of the end time. The Messiah would not only bestow the Holy Spirit, but also announce judgment. Escape from the wrath to come is possible only acknowledging and confessing one's sins. This leads to absolute reliance upon the mercies of a gracious God from which the fruits of the Spirit spring in obedient and faithful lives.

Baptism of Jesus 3:13–17

In order to launch his own mission, Jesus presents himself for baptism. John understandably questions the propriety of the request. After all, John is the prophet of the Lord while Jesus is the anointed of the Lord. John again confesses that Jesus is mightier than he (3:11). Instead of baptizing the Messiah with water, the Messiah should baptize him with the Spirit.

Jesus identifies with God's covenant people and their stead fulfills righteousness. The term involves a standard of faithfulness and obedience of life demanded by God from his people. But it also bespeaks forgiveness, bestowed as a gift of grace upon his people. Abraham believed the promise God made to him; his faith was accounted to him as righteousness (Genesis 15:6). David speaks of that righteousness in terms of iniquities being forgiven (Psalm 32:1f). Jesus' claim probably refers to obedience to the holy will of God demanded of all who by faith in his gracious promises belong to his kingdom.

Tradition and piety, grounded in Old Testament thought, postulated a great outpouring of the Spirit of God with the dawn of the messianic age. The Father pronounces Jesus to be his servant, anointed to a ministry culminating in suffering, death and resurrection (Psalm 2:7; Isaiah 42:1ff). Filled with the Holy Spirit on Pentecost, the apostles and early Christian community proclaimed as irrefutable evidence for the advent of the messianic age the fact that the God of Abraham, Isaac and Jacob glorified his servant Jesus and raised him from the dead (Acts 3:13–15).

Temptations of the Messiah 4:1–11

Matthew records three major tests to which Jesus is subjected following his baptism. They remind his readers of the temptations which Israel encountered during its wilderness trek to the land of promise (Deuteronomy 8:3). But they also proclaim the protection, which God has promised his people (Psalm 91; Deuteronomy 6:16). They also point to the striking similarity between Jesus and Moses (Deuteronomy 34:1–4; 6:13). Jesus' triumph over Satan demonstrates both his readiness and desire to carry out the mission to which his Father has called him, not one of his own choosing or preference. The Lord experienced difficult spiritual tests and trials throughout his ministry. Yet he remained faithful to his mission.

Message and Ministry 4:12–25

The imprisonment of the Baptizer (14:3–12) triggers the move from Nazareth to Capernaum on Lake Galilee. This generally regarded as the beginning of the so-called Galilean ministry. Matthew finds in this action fulfillment of Isaiah 8:23–9:1 from which he freely quotes. The prophetic word speaks of Galilee of the Gentiles. It was a region marked by a religious, cultural, ethnic and social mix. A vibrant Jewish community, which had settled in the area, was sometimes identified with the radical political Zealot movement. To remark that Jesus withdrew into Galilee may signal rejection at Nazareth. The word of God may be rejected at one place; it will be proclaimed in another!

Jesus preaches a sturdy message of repentance. He demands radical conversion of life because in his own words and deeds the kingdom of God has, in fact, come. Both his proclamation and his healing ministry announce the presence of the God with his people.

Early in this ministry the Messiah enlists his first disciples. His summons to them is the imperious demand to follow him, i.e., to learn from him and be taught by him. For Matthew it is clear that to follow Jesus is to confess him as Messiah, Son of the living God (16:16). In such faith one lives out one's life for him in total commitment (16:24f).

Discussion

1. How is John's ministry characteristically different from that of the prophets?

2. Is the baptism of John identical with that practiced by the Christian Church?

3. What is the significance of the major temptations faced by Jesus at the beginning of his public ministry?

CHAPTER THREE

The Law and the Prophets
Matthew 5:1–48

Matthew 5–7 is often said to be the so-called Sermon on the Mount, treasured by some as the real jewel of this Gospel. Strictly speaking, it is not a sermon at all. It is a collection of sayings, discourses and teachings uttered at different places, in different times and under different circumstances during the ministry of the Messiah. Matthew portrays the listening audience as comprising crowds and disciples. The parallel between Jesus and Moses is powerfully and inescapably obvious. Moses on Mt. Sinai delivers Torah to the people. Jesus on the mount teaches the messianic Torah to the people. The setting would at once remind the readers of this Gospel that the Lord God of Israel would raise up for his people a prophet like Moses whom the people must hear and heed (Deuteronomy 18:15).

Beatitudes 5:1–16

Beatitudes (Latin: *beati*; Greek: blessed) were familiar to people nurtured in Old Testament worship and piety (Psalm 1:1; 84:5–6; 128:1). Blessedness is the state of being at peace with God because one trusts in him and seeks to live in obedience to his will. Beatitudes describe the essential spiritual characteristics of a disciple of Jesus. The Christian faith centers in the life, death and resurrection of Christ. But this is never to be understood in an abstract sense as a message, which bears little or no concrete relationship to one's manner of life. For the followers of the Messiah, there is always an ethical demand. But Jesus was neither primarily a legalist nor teacher of religious ordinances. For Jesus, the gift of God always precedes the demand of God.

The Beatitudes appear to fall into distinct groups. 5:3–5 relate to Isaiah 61:1–3, for Jesus was anointed by Spirit to proclaim the Gospel to those who are spiritually poor and comfort those who are mourning. Matthew 5:6–8 promises blessing to all who long for righteousness, mercy and purity. Later, 5:9–12 relates to transition to Jesus'

interpretation of the Law. Those who, in trust toward God, live in
obedience to his will are salt and light to the world. Salt preserves and
flavors; light illumines and glows. Disciples of Jesus shine in works of
righteousness done to the glory of their Father in heaven (5:16).

Jesus and the Law of God (5:17–18)

Scribes were known and respected as Sopherim, teachers of the sacred texts. They claimed origin in Ezra, who was skilled in the Law of
Moses (Ezra 6:7; 7:12, 21). After the destruction of the Temple (587
B.C.), Jews regarded the Law as the means of retaining their religious,
cultural and ethnic identity. Scribes became official custodians and interpreters of the Mosaic Code. Pharisees (Hebrew: *parush*, separated
ones) were fiercely loyal not only to the written Law, but to the vast
body of oral tradition and commentary, which surround it.

In Hebrew thought, the Law of God was both inviolate and unable to
be reformed because it was considered everlasting. Not the smallest
point, dot, letter or detail could be altered or omitted. Believers in the
Jewish community, inspired and encouraged by the Pharisees, sought
to fulfill each stroke of the Law. Jesus had not come to abolish, dimin-
ish or radically alter either the validity of the Law or its intrinsic divine
authority. He had come to be its fulfillment (1:22; 3:15).

The phrase, the Law and the Prophets, came to be regarded as a technical term for the body of writings known as the Old Testament. In this
context, Law, known as the Torah, the foundation of Judaism, include
the first five books whose authorship was attributed to Moses. Writings known as Joshua, Judges, Samuel, Kings, the major Prophets and
the twelve minor Prophets were designated the Prophets (Nebiim).
Remaining books were given the broad title of Psalms (Kethubim).
In their use of these Scriptures, early Christians discovered a bold and
decisive prophetic witness to the birth, life, sufferings, death, resurrection, ascension and enthronement of the Messiah. Luke reports that
after the resurrection, Jesus assured certain questions disciples that his
passion and resurrection were fully in accord with the Law, Prophets
and Psalms. Repentance and forgiveness should be proclaimed in his
name to all nations (Luke 24:25–47).

The Messiah Speaks (5:19–48)

These verses have been dubbed "sentences of sacred law." Jesus provides specific instances of that righteousness which is greater than that understood by religious leaders of his day. He employs antithetical form: "You say... I say..." In so doing, he goes to the very heart of human sinfulness, the human heart! Anger, lust, and lovelessness are the basic ingredients of acts that displease God and harm the neighbor. Furthermore, a rupture in human relationships is not repaired by mere external acts. Resentment and retaliation must surrender to a love free of hostility, coercion, and self-seeking.

Above all, disciples of the Messiah honor their word, especially if substantiated by appeal to God's holy name. Swearing (not cursing) in the name of Jahweh is appropriate in a court of justice. One may even swear by heaven or Jerusalem. But people whose righteousness exceeds that produced by Pharisaic casuistry really do not need to swear oaths at all. The principle of due process defined in Exodus 21:24 and Deuteronomy 19:21 was to curb excessive retribution and revenge. Jesus clearly understands love to be the summary of the whole law of God. (Matthew 22:34–40).

The perfect love to which Jesus summons his disciples reflects the apex achievement of the human spirit and the very nature of God himself (Leviticus 19:2; Deuteronomy 19:21). The dynamic behind such love is faith or trust in the grace of God. As members of the Christian community fail to achieve perfect love, they turn to the mercy of God revealed in Christ. In him they find forgiveness and strength to strive anew.

Discussion

1. What is the difference between gift of God and demand of God?
2. Is the perfection required of followers of Jesus within human capability?
3. What is the relationship between law of God, repentance, and faith?
4. Which righteousness exceeds that of the Pharisees in Jesus' day?

CHAPTER FOUR

Living as People of God
Matthew 6 & 7

The discourse continues with various logia and concludes with the so-called Golden Rule (7:12), considered a rule of thumb directive for those committed to the law of love (5:38–48). The final section (7:13–27) treats entrance into the kingdom and summons the people of God to build upon the firm foundation provided by the words of Jesus.

Pharisaic Judaism was heralded as the most important acts of religious devotion, charity, prayer and fasting. According to an ancient rabbinical aphorism, the world is sustained by Torah, Temple worship and deeds of compassion. Qualities manifested in the life of the pious are modesty, compassion and charity. Works of charity, prayer and fasting were thought to go beyond the ordinary demands of the Law, thus earning a special reward. The Messiah does not condemn such works (5:20). He condemns a hypocritical spirit, which practices piety only for the sake of self-gratification or to achieve recognition and praise from others.

God's People are People of Piety 6:1–4; 16–18
Charitable giving of alms was a sacred duty. Trumpets were often blown in the Temple to signal the collection of alms for specific needs. Often names of donors and amounts of their gifts were published. The Messiah condemns hypocrisy, not devotional acts themselves. Works of charity are to be done for the sake of the poor and for the praise of God. The New Testament provides a noteworthy example in Cornelius, a devout man who feared God, gave alms liberally to the people and prayed to God constantly (Acts 10:2).

The one official fast day for Jews was Yom Kippur, the annual Day of Atonement prescribed in Leviticus 16. Fasting was practiced on other occasions as well. Many strict Jews made it a practice to fast twice a week. The disciples of John even questioned Jesus as to why he did not fast (9:14). The Didache, an early Christian instructional manual (c.

A.D. 100), refers to fasting on Wednesdays and Fridays. Jesus did not forbid or abrogate the custom. But those who choose to fast must not display it as a sign of righteousness. The inward joy of true repentance and faith is far more important than any external act.

Christian piety flows from a faith relationship with the Savior. Whether you eat or drink or whatever you do, exhorts St. Paul, do it to the glory of God (1 Corinthians 10:31). The kingdom of God is righteousness, peace and joy in the Holy Spirit, not food or drink (Romans 14:17). In fact, one is to not judge another with regard to food or drink or festivals or special days (Colossians 2:16). Christian believers do all in the name of the Lord Jesus, giving thanks to God the Father through him (Colossians 3:17).

God's People are People of Prayer 6:5–15; 7:7–12
Prayer has always been an essential characteristic of the worshipping community. Psalms and liturgical prayers were an integral part of Temple and synagogue services. Fixed hours of prayer had become an accepted part of Jewish piety (Daniel 6:10). Jesus criticizes the improper use of prayer, whether it takes the form of showiness or wordiness.

The Lord's Prayer 6:9–13
Christian worship early incorporated prayer as an expression of faith and piety (Acts 2:42; Colossians 3:16f). Jesus provides a prayer to be used by God's people. The Didache directs Christians to pray the Our Father daily, a practice most likely corresponding to the Jewish custom of praying morning, afternoon and evening. The Lord's Prayer is more than a liturgical formula; it is a guide to proper prayer, which is to avoid thoughtless repetition of words. The very form of address, Our Father, reveals love and concern for God's people. Jesus himself hallowed God's name as he proclaimed the good news (Gospel) of the kingdom, which had come in his own ministry. The Messiah is the ultimate deliverance from every evil of body and spirit.

God's People are People of Trust 6:19–7:23
Discipleship is revealed in relation to material goods (6:19–23) and to the concerns of everyday living (6:24–34). God's redeemed people

demonstrate single-minded devotion as they live in absolute trust in God as their good and gracious Father in Christ.

In Jesus' age and culture, wealth was measured largely in terms of land, luxurious clothing, sumptuous food stores, building and costly household items such as wood and iron chests. In that day, such treasures were particularly subject to specific perils such as moth, rust (or worm) and robbery. Jesus accords the name, mammon (Aramaic: *mamona*, riches), to clothing, food property, pleasure, possessions and anything else that becomes an object of worship of trust.

Furthermore, worry, anxiety and fear attend the confidence one places in earthly treasures and goods. They are transient. True treasures, by contrast, consist in spiritual wealth: peace, forgiveness, joy, confidence of grace, assurance, commitment and trust in the promises of God. These endure because they are bestowed by the Holy Spirit. Jesus postulates a simple rule: Where your treasure is, there your heart will be (6:21). Whenever one prays, Our Father in heaven, decision has been made in favor of God over mammon. Seeking that righteousness, which is both a gift from God and demand of God, frees the believer to live without anxious and troublesome thoughts, which rob the heart and peace

Built on the Rock 7:13–29

Not everyone who purports to be a member of the Messianic community actually belongs to it. Obedience to the Father in heaven is the genuine fruit of faith and commitment. Jesus point particularly to false and deceptive claims of charismatic endowment. In the final judgment, many who had nothing more than an external relationship to Christ will refer to prophecy, miracles and exorcisms performed in the Messiah's name. The Lord will reject as lawless workers of iniquity all who acted contrary to the will of God. Those who truly trust in God as Father do greater works of loving obedience to his will (6:33; 7:12, 21).

Above all, the people of God hear and rely upon the words of the Messiah. They are the truly wise who know that a firm, solid foundation is necessary if faith is to survive. In this Gospel, reference is often made to people of little faith (6:30; 8:26; 14:31; 16:8; 17:20; 21:21–23). Followers and disciples of Jesus are called to great faith. Faith in the mercies of God revealed in Jesus Christ are not mere knowledge, not mere words that one may speak about Christ. Faith is trust in his life, death and resurrection. Faith always builds upon that foundation.

On Christ the solid rock I stand
All other ground is sinking sand!

Discussion

1. Is the "golden rule" unique to biblical teaching? Do other religions have it?

2. Is the Lord's Prayer for all people or just for Christians? To whom did our Lord teach it?

3. What are features of God-pleasing prayer in light of Jesus' teachings?

Conclusion

With precise clarity and insight, the author of this First Gospel witnesses and shares, particularly with Judaism, the deep and abiding conviction of the Christian community: Jesus is Messiah and Savior. He is conceived and born in fulfillment of ancient prophecies made to Israel. He is acknowledged and given due homage by Magi from the east as the revelation of Yahweh to Gentile nations. His ministry is heralded and introduced by John the Baptizer, latter day Elijah whose own ministry is to prepare God's people for their Messiah. He receives at his baptism attestation from the heaven that he is the Anointed One. He successfully withstands severe tests by Satan, which would thwart his mission and ministry. He executes his Messianic role in fulfillment of Law and Prophets. He upholds the authority of Torah. At the same time, he assumes the prerogative and reinterpretation for the community, which confesses him as Lord. He provides positive directives for living as the people of God. He challenges his hearers build both faith and life upon the solid, immovable foundation of his word. He demands of them a righteousness, which exceeds the casuistic legalism imposed by Scribes and Pharisees (5:20).

As Matthew concludes, his record of the assorted discourses, which some like to group together as the Sermon on the Mount, he observes that those who attentively listen to these sayings are profoundly amazed. They realize that Jesus teaches with an authority, which they have not experienced, from their own religious leaders. Matthew continues his narrative as he further witnesses to the authority and mission of the Messiah.

Part Two

Authority and Mission of the Messiah

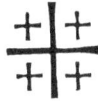

+|+
+|+

This section of the Gospel stresses the authority that Jesus has to execute his mission. He is the revelation of the Father and is confessed by his closest companions and disciples to be the Son of the living God. As such he is the true shepherd of Israel. His glory is beheld high upon the Mount of Transfiguration. He triumphantly enters the ancient royal city and is acclaimed both David's son, true king of Israel and also David's Lord. But the authority of Messiahship calls for commitment of discipleship. Jesus challenges his hearers to follow him. The genuine disciple steps out from the faceless crowds to pledge personal commitment, which results from faith in the saving words of the Lord.

CHAPTER FIVE

Authority of the Messiah
Matthew 8:1–9:38

In countless instances recorded by Matthew, Jesus possesses and exercises Messianic authority (7:29; 8:2–3; 26–27; 9:6, 8; 28–29). Matthew carefully notes that the Roman centurion whose servant Jesus
heals is an officer under commanding authority. He recognizes the
greater authority in Jesus. The Messiah takes this opportunity to declare that Gentiles will participate in the great banquet of salvation
with Abraham, Isaac and Jacob (Cf. 22:1–14).

Ministry of Healing 8:1–34; 9:18–34

In masterful interweaving of miracle and discipleship narratives, Matthew claims Jesus' rule over the realms of the physical, demonic and
natural. Three stories constitute the first grouping, conclusively dem-
onstrating healing power over leprosy, paralysis and fever. The author
is also concerned that the first miracles involve a Jew, a Gentile and a
member of a disciple's family. His mission is to all. Ritual purification
was the domain of Temple priests (Leviticus 13–14). Cleansing of lepers was a sign to the Messianic age (11:5). The Messiah does not over-
turn Mosaic regulations. He had come to fulfill the Law (5:17), just as
he fulfills the prophetic words of Isaiah 53:4, which describes the role
and mission of God's servant.

Following Jesus entails much more than moving with him from place
to place. It spells out commitment. A certain Scribe desires to become
a rabbinical student. A certain disciple wants to follow but first must
attend to burial rites. Jesus is not insensitive to human obligations. But
he wants to impress upon all would-be recruits the hardship, loneliness, sacrifice and single-minded devotion involved in being a true
disciple of the Lord.

In the mouth of Jesus, the title, Son of Man, is a potent reminder that
in him God's reign has most assuredly come. He has dominion and

power, which are neither transient nor temporal, though his ministry bears the marks of humiliation and suffering. One must avoid all forms of procrastination in heeding Jesus' call for decision (16:24–28). Those who pledge absolute commitment to him will reign with him (Daniel 7:13–18).

Three miracle narratives constitute the second grouping made by Matthew. Stilling the storm is viewed as both miracle and discipleship narrative. Messiah's people will be swamped by storms of adversity and waves of trial. Disciples will know that their Lord is always with them (28:20) on life's tempestuous seas. Early Christian art and literature often depicts the Church as a ship tossed by seas of adversity and persecution, preserved by Christ, the master helmsman.

The incident of healing in Gentile territory may have overtones of Isaiah 65:1–8. Demons acknowledge Jesus as Son of God, possessed of power since he was anointed by the Spirit of God. On Hebrew thought, satanic forces will be finally destroyed in the great Day of Judgment. The messianic reign (12:28) will come to final and sublime fulfillment when the Son of God, who is also the Son of Man, comes in his glory (25:31–46).

Ministry of Forgiveness 9:1–17

Jesus extends his authority from the realm of creation and physical illness to the realm of sin. Biblical thought sees sin, violation of God's holy will, as the ultimate cause of creation's bondage to corruption, decay, sickness and death. Jesus returns to Capernaum where commenced his ministry (4:12–17). Jesus notes the faith of friends who bear the paralytic to him. More importantly, he goes to the very heart of the problem as he absolves the man from sin. To his religious detractors, this compassionate act was nothing less than blatant usurpation of God's prerogative. It constituted blasphemy. Jesus answers their as yet unspoken charge by curing the man of paralysis. Healing in this instance is evidence not only of forgiveness, but also of divine authority. He who will act as judge on the great day of the Lord is exercising that judgment in the acquittal of the sinner by means of his word.

Scribes and Pharisees reproach Jesus for eating with custom officials and other members of society who ignored many of the customs, rites and requirements imposed by religious legalists. Jesus came to minister to the spiritually sick and extend his forgiveness to them. He is the bridegroom inviting guests to the messianic wedding banquet. That is why he and his disciples do not fast. It is incongruous to inject signs of mourning into the joy of forgiveness and the new life, which it brings.

Matthew resumes his account with a group of four miracle narratives (9:18–34). Healing of the woman is joined to that of the ruler's daughter. Resurrection from death is the ultimate healing. It demonstrates absolute authority over the realm of the physical. It also serves to presage Jesus' own resurrection from the dead (28:6–7). The last two healings are strongly suggestive of Isaiah 34:6 (Cf. also 29:18 and 35:5). Healing of blindness is a mark of divine power (Isaiah 42:7; 61:1). In faith, the blind men "see" what the Lord's adversaries fail to see.

Sheep Without a Shepherd 9:35–38

By means of this transitional material, Matthew brings the miracle and discipleship narratives to conclusion. He asserts once again the messianic authority enjoyed by Jesus. At the beginning of his public ministry, Jesus summons disciples to follow him. He goes into Galilee teaching, preaching and healing (4:23) as one who has authority (7:28). Now he will commit this authority to the Twelve who are commissioned to share his ministry with multitudes who are virtually shepherdless. Reference to harvest is most likely allusive to judgment as in Isaiah 9:2–3; 17:11; 27:12. In the parables recorded by Matthew (13:24–39), harvest is a symbol of judgment. Israel is given opportunity to return to its true shepherd (Isaiah 40:10–11; Psalm 23:1; Ezekiel 34:11) as it repents and receives from Christ the gospel of the kingdom. That is why Jesus sends his ambassadors to the lost sheep of the house of Israel.

Discussion

1. What is the healing ministry of the contemporary church?
2. Is forgiving sins an exclusively divine prerogative? Under what, if any, circumstances may a human being absolve?
3. What kind of "authority" is a sure sign of the Messianic age?

CHAPTER SIX

Apostleship and Discipleship
Matthew 10:1–42

Matthew has conclusively established the authority of Jesus. On this authority, the Messiah commissions disciples to preach the good news (3:2; 4:17), heal the sick, raise the dead, cleanse the lepers and cast out demons. People without shepherds are provided new spiritual shepherds in the persons of the apostles.

Names of the Twelve Apostles 10:1–31

Simon Peter
Andrew
James
John
Philip
Bartholomew
Thomas
Matthew
James Thaddeus
Simon
Judas

To this point, Matthew has recorded the call of five (4:18–22; 9:9). He does not describe the formal appointment of the additional seven. The very number, twelve, reminds Israel that twelve tribes (19:28) constituted its nation. Jewish synagogues may also have been governed by councils of twelve elders. For the first time, Matthew bestows upon those chosen the technical title, apostle, i.e., sent out ones who are emissaries of the Messiah.

While this Gospel leaves little question that the tax-collector, known as a publican (Latin: *publicani*, handler of public money), called to follow Jesus bears the name Matthew, both Mark and Luke know him as Levi. Mark even identifies him as the son of Alphaeus (Mark 3:18).

This might even make him a brother of the second James who appears in the apostolic list. Others suggest that he is really Matthew ben Levi, i.e., the son of Levi. It was common for people of the time to have both an Aramaic and Greek name. Peter is known by his Aramaic name, Cephas; Thomas is called Didymus (Greek: twin).

Other than that contained in the New Testament, we posses little reliable information concerning the apostles. Numerous legends and traditions regarding their life and ministry grew up in the early Church. It is probably safe to assume that most of them labored in Jerusalem and among Jewish Christians who dispersed from the city particularly after A.D. 70. Peter appears to have exercised early leadership in the Jerusalem congregation, which elected Matthias to replace Judas Iscariot (Acts 1:12–26). Later James plays that role (Acts 15:13–22). The other James, brother of John, is presumed to be the first martyred (Acts 12:1–2). Tradition has it that all except John experienced similar martyrdom. Reports that several of the apostles were married are undoubtedly accurate. The wife of Peter is said to have accompanied him and died as a martyr for the faith. Philip is said to have had several daughters. One church historian speaks of the grandsons of Jude, whose wife was Mary. A fairly reliable tradition places Andrew in Asia Minor and Greece, although a richly fanciful legend connects him with the work of Matthew in Ethiopia or Persia. Bartholomew, known also as Nathaneal, preached in Armenia, while Thomas founded the church in India where he became a powerful witness to the resurrection of the Lord. Simon and Jude labored in Egypt and Persia. John located in Ephesus where he died a natural death c. A.D. 100.

The apostles share the peace and blessings of the kingdom. Whenever the word of God is proclaimed, peace is offered; whenever that word is spurned, peace is rejected. Such rejection evokes judgment greater than that, which befell Sodom and Gomorrah. Though the apostles are sent to shepherdless flocks, they will feel that they are sheep sent in among wolves. They will be subjected to persecution simply because they proclaim the gospel. Jesus promises that God will be their defense. They are in the hands of the same Father who anointed Jesus with the Holy Spirit and with power (Acts 10:38).

Confessing Christ as Lord 10:32–42

The mission, ministry and message of the Messiah form a cutting edge, which separates those who acknowledge his as Lord from those who deny him; those who love him above all else from those who love him less; those who are ready to bear the cross for him from those who are not; those who desire to follow him from those who do not. Some, remaining faithful to the Gospel, will sacrifice physical life for him; they are certain of life in the age to come. Some, denying Christ and the Gospel, will preserve physical life, only ultimately to lose that life promised by Christ.

Matthew does not directly like this unequivocal demand of discipleship to Jesus' own suffering and death (16:21). Yet the allusion is obvious. It is almost as though Jesus sends the disciples out with the shadow of Calvary cast over them. Discipleship is never easy. Confessing Christ as Lord entails self-denial, suffering and readiness to follow him to one's own Calvary of loneliness, opposition and self-sacrifice.

Matthew makes no reference to the return of the apostles. Neither does he comment on the success or failure of their mission. He concludes this missionary discourse with the potent reminder that whoever welcomes an apostle of the Lord welcomes the Lord himself. Yahweh commissioned his prophets during the Old Testament dispensation. Yahweh's Anointed has commissioned the apostles. Those who hear their message must decide for or against it. Decision for Christ is where true discipleship always begins.

Discussion

1. What is the difference between a disciple and an apostle?

2. What does it really mean for one to confess that Jesus is both Lord and Christ?

3. What does confessing Jesus actually entail?

CHAPTER SEVEN

Jesus, Revelation of the Father
Matthew 11:1–12:50

In establishing Messianic claims and authority for Jesus of Nazareth, Matthew has stressed important themes to which his hearers would be particularly sensitive. He has pointed out that Jesus is greater than Moses, through whom God gave Torah to Israel. Jesus is the fulfillment of all Old Testament prophecy. Jesus is both fulfiller and interpreter of Torah, the Law of God. Jesus' own ministry, as well as his authority to commission apostles to preach and teach, flow from these claims. Furthermore, his call to follow him in discipleship and confess him as Lord are unmistakable signs of divine prerogative.

Matthew returns to one of his basic themes. Jesus is not only greater than Moses; he is greater than John the Baptizer, greater than Satan, greater than the prophet Jonah, greater than the mighty King Solomon. Even more compelling, Jesus is greater than the Temple, greater than Sabbath laws, greater than Israel herself. Jesus does the works foretold in Isaiah 35:5–6, proclaims the message described in Isaiah 61:1–3 and fulfills the prophecy of Isaiah 42:1–4. Beyond all question, he is the Messiah, revelation of the Father.

Jesus is the Coming One 11:1–30

The designation, Coming One, already applied by John (3:11), is possibly drawn from Isaiah 59:20, a passage frequently read in the synagogue services. In the ministry of Jesus, Yahweh's day of salvation has come. People may use different means, even violent ones, in abortive attempts to force the coming of God's kingdom. Some resort to signs and miracles and prophecies, claiming that Christ has already returned or given them privileged information as to date, time and location – in spite of Jesus' own clear warnings regarding deceit in his name (Cf. 24:23–36). Revolutionaries of Jesus' time sought to establish God's kingdom on earth by forceful insurrection against the Roman government. Pharisees attempted to take the kingdom by force as they resolutely persecuted all who dared proclaim Jesus as Messiah and Lord. God's kingdom comes in the wisdom and power of God, not by human initiative or ingenuity. It appeared in the Messiah, whose coming was prepared by the ministry of John. Those who rejected that ministry and the subsequent ministry of Jesus, will be denied by the Messiah in the Day of Judgment. This give added weight to the solemn admonition to hear him.

The powerful words which follow the directive to hear the Messiah's words (11:15) constitute a prayer, a claim and an invitation. Some have dubbed these words a thunderbolt out of the blue because of their markedly decisive character and content. Cities of Galilee, places where Jesus performed most of his works, will fail to recognize them as signs that God's kingdom is in their midst. Those who are, or claim to be, wise in their own understanding will fail to confess that Jesus is the Lord's Anointed. Nonetheless the kingdom of God comes, despite opposition and rejection. Some will hear and take to heart the message of peace and salvation, which the Messiah brings. Jesus thanks his Father in heaven for revealing the mystery of the kingdom to childlike disciples.

Matthew expands his theme of the Messiah's absolute uniqueness as revealer of God. All things are delivered to him by the Father (28:20). All truth has been transmitted from the Father to the Son. No one really knows the Son except the Father; no one really knows the Father except his Son and those to whom the Son reveals him. Therefore, it follows that in the Son alone God's people may find comfort and relief from the burdensome and restrictive rules and regulations imposed upon them by their spiritual leaders. Through the Son, God gives the Holy Spirit so that his people hear and believe his revelation. They are empowered to live the life of righteousness, which surpasses that of the Scribes and Pharisees (5:20).

Jesus Christ is Lord 12:1–50

As Jesus exercises messianic authority opposition on the part of the Pharisaic party continues to grown in extent and intensity. He who is greater than Moses demonstrates that he is Lord of the Sabbath. Part of Mosaic Law, Sabbath observance was a weekly reminder of God's creation of the world in six days (Genesis 1). Scribes and Pharisees in particular viewed Sabbath regulations as a sign of the Covenant of Yahweh with his people. The very notion of Sabbath rest was also a foretoken of that eternal rest of the people of God. The writer of Hebrews (4:1–11) links the attainment of the rest with the preaching of the gospel.

All Jews looked upon the Sabbath as nothing less than a holy treasure given to Israel by its Redeemer (Exodus 20). Priests might serve in the Temple on the Sabbath; special works deemed necessary to preserve life might be performed. All other work was strictly forbidden. Observance of Sabbath was a hallmark of Judaism. The action of the disciples was therefore considered to be a serious breach of the Law (Exodus 34:21). Jesus counters the accusations of the Pharisees by alluding to the well-known story of David which is recounted in I Samuel 21:1–6. But he goes beyond the example of David and the Temple priests. A greater than the Temple is in their midst. The Son of Man and his disciples have not only the same privilege accorded to Old Testament priests; he who is greater than the Temple is in fact the great High Priest who was to come. Furthermore, there is a law higher than ritual, regulation, even sacrifice. The law of mercy supercedes (Hosea 6:6; Matthew 5:7; 43–38). Besides that, the Son of Man is Lord of the Sabbath since his authority extends over the whole Law of God.

Controversy over the Sabbath continues in the synagogue. Matthew wants his readers to be fully aware of the sharpening of opposition between disciples of the Messiah (12:2), representatives of the New Israel and Pharisees who represent the old. As Pharisees question Jesus concerning healing on the Sabbath, Jesus refers to the accepted principle that Sabbath regulations permit works of mercy and love. God desires them (22:39–40). The Messiah who has come to fulfill the Law acts according to God's will. The miracle of healing provides conclusive evidence that the heavy burden of regulation, restriction and ritual is to be exchanged for the light yoke of obedience to the new Torah Jesus delivers.

The Pharisees fully understand what Jesus is saying (12:14). The dye is cast. Jesus continues his healing ministry in fulfillment of Isaiah 42:1–4. This lengthy quotation is neither an exact rendering of the Hebrew nor the Greek text of Isaiah. But it stresses the role of the servant anointed with the Spirit to proclaim righteousness and victory.

It also reminds the reader of the voice from heaven at the baptism of Jesus (3:13–17). As Israel turns away from God's Messiah, Gentiles will turn to him in whom the kingdom has erupted. Old Israel is rejecting his ministry. It has become an evil and adulterous generation, unfaithful to Yahweh and his covenant. In willful blindness to signs, which the Holy Spirit is revealing, it keeps on requesting signs (12:30–39).

At Pentecost, as Jesus had promised the disciples, the Holy Spirit was poured out upon the Christian community. The Spirit testifies to the life, death and resurrection of Jesus. As people reject this witness of the Holy Spirit and even blaspheme the Spirit of God who would bring them into the messianic realm of forgiveness, peace and joy, they commit the sin that is beyond forgiveness.

Jesus will provide one sign – that of the prophet Jonah. This is usually interpreted to prefigure the death of Jesus as well as the judgment, which his preaching is executing. Jesus will offer up his like. God will raise him from the dead. Filled with genuine Pentecostal zeal and confidence, the apostles boldly proclaimed that the God of Abraham, Isaac and Jacob glorified his servant Jesus. You delivered him up, they testified. You denied the holy and righteous one. You killed the author of life. But God raised him. We are witnesses (Acts 3:13–15). God exalted Jesus at his own right hand to give repentance to Israel and forgiveness of sins. We are witnesses to this. So it the Holy Spirit (Acts 5:30–32).

Matthew concludes this section of his testimony with the chilling words of Jesus directed to the perverse generation with which he was dealing. Discipleship is never a matter of proper birth, social position, cultural heritage, spiritual prerogative or circumstance, which are quite accidental. The family of the Messiah is those who attentively hear his words and follow him in faith. They constitute the New Israel, which by spiritual rebirth confesses that Jesus is indeed greater than King David, greater than the prophet Jonah and greater than any heritage of which one might boast. In such conviction and commitment they seek to do the will of God.

Discussion

1. Note the literary technique by which Matthew stresses the role of Jesus in revealing the Father.

2. Review the important role played in Hebrew life and worship by the Sabbath.

3. Do "signs" always unmistakably point to God's presence and works? Are there such things as false signs? How do we test signs to see if they are genuine?

CHAPTER EIGHT

The Kingdom of God
Matthew 13:1–52

The disciples of Jesus have received the kingdom of God because knowledge of its secrets has been reveled to them. The phrase, secrets of the kingdom, was well known in Hebrew literature and tradition. It refers to divine mysteries known only by those privileged to understand them. This insight has been given to the disciples by the Lord of heaven and earth through his Son Jesus, the Messiah (11:25–27).

Spiritual perception and understanding are always a gift of the Holy Spirit. It is bestowed so that faith, which clings to Christ and his promise of forgiveness and peace, might ever stand in the power of God, not in human wisdom (Cf. I Corinthians 2:1–12). Old Israel, represented by teachers such as the Scribes and Pharisees, neither listens to the Messiah nor perceives what he is saying. New Israel, represented by disciples and apostles, both listens and grasps the significance of what he is saying.

Matthew continues his record of the mission and ministry of the Messiah by reporting the form of teaching adopted by Jesus known as parable. In resorting to parables, Jesus fulfills the prophecy of Isaiah 6:9–20. Parables (Hebrew: *mashal*, proverb; Greek: a literary form of simile or comparison) have been defined as simple, consistent, often pithy and effective expositions of spiritual truths by means of simile or likeness drawn from mundane things. The parables of Jesus are not simple (or even complex) religious vignettes whose purpose is to entertain universal spiritual or ethical principles. In the New Testament, parables illustrate truths directly linked with the kingdom, which has been inaugurated in the person, life, works, words, passion and resurrection of the Messiah. Reflecting his fondness for numbers, Matthew selects seven parables spoken by Jesus. They enunciate the universality of the kingdom, describe discipleship in the kingdom and identify the true Israel of God. Matthew is careful to assert that Jesus spoke parables to great crowds gathered outside the house (13:1–35). Special instruction is given to his disciples inside the house (13:36–52). The symbolism is telling. True followers of the Messiah are inside the kingdom. Acknowledging the truth that Jesus is the revelation of God's saving will toward humankind they understand the mysteries of the kingdom of God.

Parable of the Sower 13:1–23

Seed strewn by the sower falls on various kinds of soil. Some ground is hard trodden, some is rocky and some is thorn-filled. But some is rich, loamy, thorn-free soil. God's kingdom has erupted in the ministry of Jesus. John proclaimed it. Disciples and apostles were commissioned to witness it. Opposition on the part of the religious leaders of the day reached a point of rupture.

Every sower knows the difficulties, frustrations, anxieties and failures connected with such work. Sowing the word of the kingdom is similarly fraught with difficulty and frustration. In spite of this, the work of the kingdom continues as words of Jesus are spread and fall on the hearts of their hearers. The word, which proclaims redemption and salvation in the life, death and resurrection of Jesus Christ calls for repentance and faith and decision. Thee will be loss and failure. But thee will also be rich harvest. Success is promised. The word of the Gospel bears abundant fruit as the people of God confess Jesus as Lord and seek to do the will of his Father in heaven.

Parable of the Wheat and Weeds 13:24–30; 36–43

Jesus teaches parabolic truths just as Moses taught in the desert (Exodus 19:7). Those who constitute his kingdom, in response to his work, are to bear abundant fruit. Sometimes people identify with the messianic community, but fail to produce fruits and works of faith. In ancient Palestine, a poisonous weed was barely distinguishable from wheat. Its roots were exceptionally strong. Pulling weeds out of the field would frequently uproot good croup of wheat, especially when shoots of wheat were young and tender. Farmers often wisely let weeds and wheat grow together. At harvest the reaper would cut both grain and weeds. Weeds would then be gathered to provide fuel.

Harvest and fire often serve as metaphors for judgment (Jeremiah

51:53) and signs of separation. People, who for any number of reasons are drawn into the external fellowship of the Church, but who do not inwardly confess Jesus as Lord, are fickle, not faithful. Outwardly they may resemble those who conform to the strict demands of discipleship, but they do not measure up. One does not immediately root them out as worthless weeds. The fickle grow with the faithful. But the day of separation and judgment surely comes. The Son of Man, at the close of the age, separates weeds from wheat, fickle from faithful. The righteous, those who have found forgiveness in Christ, shine in the kingdom, as possible allusion to the day of resurrection in Daniel 12:3. Identification with the community of Christ is a most serious matter. It calls for earnest discipleship, not mere acquaintanceship; it summons to faithfulness, not fickleness. Listen, all who have ears of spiritual discernment!

Parable of the Mustard Seed 13:31–32

Sowing the seed of the Gospel is met by setback and failure. Weeds grow along with the good grain. Sometimes the kingdom appears to be so very small and unpretentious; it appears to have little power or influence on earth. We pray, the kingdom come, yet it comes apparently to so few. We are so prone to judge by purely human standards. The kingdom, says Jesus, is like a grain of mustard seed. It may be the smallest and most unimposing of all seeds. But its potential for growth is enormous. In Palestine it was quite normal for a mustard tree to attain height of one to twelve feet. It could provide lodging for many birds (Cf. Daniel 4:7–24). In Hebrew literature, the phrase, birds of heaven, commonly symbolized Gentile nations (Ezekiel 31:6). The kingdom of the Messiah reaches into all the world (Matthew 28:19ff).

Parable of the Leaven 13:33

Once yeast is worked into dough, it permeates the mixture until all has been leavened. The kingdom of the Messiah may be hidden in the sense that it began with little outward show. An obscure prophet wearing camel's hair began to preach repentance in the wilderness of Judea (3:2). Another relatively obscure man from Nazareth received his baptism and began to proclaim the advent of the kingdom (4:17). Disciples gathered about him and apostles were commissioned by him to go out into all the world (28:1ff). Let loose in the world, the kingdom grows and will continue to grow under adverse circumstances, losses, disappointments, setbacks and failures. After all, it is God's kingdom, not ours!

Parable of the Treasure 13:44

Parables of Jesus are not ethical maxims or norms to serve as moral guidelines for society. The moral quality or legality of the man's actions is not the point of this parable. When a person is brought into the kingdom by faith in Jesus Christ an overwhelming decision has been made. It so fills one with joy that one is ready to part with whatever is necessary to retain the kingdom of God and its blessings. To do otherwise is unthinkable. Christ is the choicest possession one can own.

Parable of the Pearl 13:45–46

The identical point is the thrust and purpose of this next closely related parable. The magnificence of the pearl is such that one is ready and willing to part with everything else in order to possess it. God's kingdom, like God's Word, is better than thousands of gold and silver pieces (Psalm 119:72). Gain from proper wisdom and understanding is better than gain from silver and gold. Divine wisdom is more precious than all jewels (Proverbs 3:13–15).

Parable of the Good and Worthless Fish 13:47–50

Matthew concludes this discourse on the kingdom, not surprisingly, with a parable, which stresses final judgment. It is almost a reprise of the parable of weeds and wheat. Separation is inevitable. People must make a decision to enter the kingdom of the Messiah. They must continue to commit themselves to discipleship and all that it entails. Every teacher of Torah who has become a disciple of Jesus fully understands that. Those who continue to cling to the philosophy of the Pharisees utterly fail to comprehend that the new age has dawned. They take offense at the Messiah and reject his ministry. Sadly, to them he always was and will be little more than the carpenter's son from Nazareth. Their unbelief blinds them to his person, words, claims and works. Separation has, in fact, already occurred. Those who have become part of the messianic community of faith have stepped out of the Pharisaic community of unbelief.

Matthew records additional parables spoken by Jesus. He also records various sayings of Jesus, which describe the community, which confesses him as Lord. Both are found in segments, which a number of commentators refer to as constituting the second major part of this Gospel because of their contextual setting. There is, to be sure, a decided shift in both emphasis and mood. The mission and ministry of the Messiah were met with absolute rejection on the part of Pharisaic Judaism. Not Matthew will depict the mission of Jesus in terms of the cross, i.e., in terms of suffering and death to which rejection will ultimately lead him.

Discussion

1. What does it mean to be part of the kingdom of God? How does one enter it?

2. Parables form a large part of our Savior's teaching ministry. Why is a parable an effective literary tool? Is there a "key" that opens the reader/hearer to proper understanding?

3. Are the parables of Jesus similar to Aesop's fables? Are they all "true" stories?

CHAPTER NINE

Son of the Living God
Matthew 14:1–17–23

The ministry of the Messiah has been depicted in teaching, preaching, healing and commissioning disciples and apostles to carry on his work in his name. As opposition to his mission increases, those who confess him as the long-awaited Redeemer of Israel must be assured and reassured that he truly is Son of the Living God. At the same time they must be led to realize that divine Sonship and Messiahship do not preclude the cross.

Matthew records predictions and allusions, which point to the impending passion of the Lord. The murder of John, forerunner of the Messiah, is depicted as the death of a prophet (14:5). Jesus warns his disciples that he must suffer many things from the religious hierarchy of Israel and be killed (16:21). After the faith-strengthening experience of the Transfiguration, Jesus confides that the Son of Man is to be delivered into the hands of those who will put him to death, but he will be raised on the third day (17:12). Jesus pronounces a woe upon the spiritual heirs of those who shed the blood of the Old Testament prophets. Their generation will crucify another of God's prophets, the Messiah himself (23:29–38). In addition to these clear words of witness to his passion, Jesus defines discipleship in terms of denial and taking up the cross in order to follow him (16:24).

Death of John the Baptizer 14:1–12

Herod Antipas, son of Herod the Great, ruled my imperial favor as tetrarch over Galilee and Perea. His second marriage to Herodias was forbidden by Jewish law (Leviticus 20:21). When John denounced Herod's scandalous sin, he was imprisoned in the dungeon fortress of Machaerus, located on the eastern side of the Dead Sea. Herod was vain and callous. Incited by his teenage stepdaughter's (Salome) suggestive dance, Herod makes a rash promise. He fulfills it at the insistence of his wife. John's death anticipates the approaching death of Jesus.

As rumors regarding the ministry of Jesus spread, superstitious, fear-crazed and conscience-tormented Herod believes that the Baptizer has risen from the dead. The doctrine of resurrection was firmly held and taught by the sect of Pharisees as a correct understanding of Old Testament teaching. Occurrences of resurrection were, in fact, widely interpreted as signs of the Messianic age (27:51–53). In recording the mistaken belief of Herod, Matthew may well be pointing to the actual resurrection of the Messiah (28:5–6), which fulfills the Son of Man's prediction (16:21).

True Shepherd of Israel 14:13–16:12

Six accounts of miraculous multiplication of loaves are recorded in the Gospels. Feeding the multitudes in the desert is strongly reminiscent of the feeding of Israel during its wilderness trek from Egypt to Canaan (Exodus 16:1–16). Bread is symbolic of the word with which God feeds and nourishes the spiritual life of his people. The incident points to Jesus' response to Satan: We do not live by bread alone, but by the word which God speaks (4:4). The Gospel according to John records precise words of Jesus in which he claims to be living bread from heaven (John 6:48–51).

As dispenser of the bread of life, Jesus feeds and leads God's people into the rich pasture of God's word. A true shepherd feeds Israel with un-leavened bread of truth. False shepherds feed Israel leavened bread of lies, deceit and hypocrisy. Such food can never satisfy spiritual hunger or nourish spiritual life. That is why Jesus has come. For the scattered, hungry and faint, Jesus supplies in abundance bread, which truly satis-fies their spiritual yearnings.

The Messiah multiplies, blesses, breaks and gives the loaves to the dis-ciples. They, in turn, distribute them to the crowds (14:19; 15:36). This reflects a daily and well-known action in a Jewish household. The father takes bread, gives thanks, breaks it and shares it with the members of the family. Servants would often assist in the distribution. These significant words reappear in the Eucharistic formula (26:26). The entire action pre-figures the banquet of salvation at which God's people participate with the Messiah in the feast of eternal life.

The twelve baskets of fragments focus attention on the twelve apostles as representatives of the twelve tribes of Israel. The blessings and care of Jesus extend to the whole people of God. In striking contrast, feeding of four thousand takes place in a predominantly Gentile region. Seven baskets are gathered. Gentiles will share in the feast of salvation as they sit with God's Messiah at a table with Abraham, Isaac and Jacob (8:11).

The community, which confesses Jesus as Son of God, faces hardship, difficulty and fear. The community to which and for which Matthew writes has already experienced such. As a ship beaten by wind and wave many furlongs distant from the safety of harbor or shore, God's people encounter doubts, anxieties and littleness of faith. The true Shepherd of Israel does not leave or forsake his own. He comes to them, even in the fourth watch of the night (between 3:00–6:00 A.M.) to assure them of his mighty presence. He is master of wind and wave. His people witness the truth that before him no God was formed, nor shall be after him. He is Lord! Beside him there is no Savior (Isaiah 43:10–11). Whenever the community cries out with Peter, Lord save me, the Savior reaches out to deliver. Truly he is Messiah and Son of God, a conviction, which anticipates the confession of Peter (16:16) and the witnessing voice from heaven (17:5).

Jesus is also Lord of that body of Hebrew tradition later known as Mishnah (Hebrew: repetition). Produced by rabbis and scholars, Mishnah was composed during the two centuries of the Christian era. Along with Gemara (Hebrew: completion), Mishnah forms the Talmud, primary source of Jewish commentary on Torah. Scribes and Pharisees accorded Mishnah equal importance and authority with the Mosaic code. Ever alert for the slightest infraction of their religious rules, Pharisees demand to know why Jesus permits his followers to disregard a solemn tradition (15:1–2). He who is Lord of Sabbath asks why they are ready to violate a written command of God regarding care of parents (Exodus 12:20). Their base hypocrisy is characterized by Isaiah 29:13. They reveal that they are blind leaders, unfaithful shepherds who mask the clear will of God by means of their own rigid notions of religiosity. Failure to observe ceremonial ablutions does not defile. One is defile by imperfect thoughts (5:48). Worst of all, these religious leaders utterly fail to understand that love is the supreme commandment. It is superior to all tradition (22:38–40).

Messiah further demonstrates lordship over tradition as he trans-
fers his ministry to the Phoenician coastal cities of Tyre and Sidon
(15:21). Jesus severely tests the faith of a Canaanite woman. In select-
ing this particular narrative, Matthew attests what for his Jewish readers was a truly revolutionary precept. Gentiles can share both the faith
and privileges of the new Israel. Moreover, they may possess truly great
faith. As Messiah Jesus is prepared to break with any tradition, which
might impede his mission to all the nations (28:18–20). As he continues his ministry of healing among non-Jewish settlements (4:12–18)
bordering the eastern shore of the Sea of Galilee, multitudes glorify
the God of Israel. They perceive what the false shepherds in their stubborn blindness simply could not perceive.

Jesus Christ, Son of the Living God 16:13–17:27

Some twenty-five miles north of the sea lay Caesarea Philippi, built
and named in honor of the Roman Emperor. There Jesus asks the truly
pivotal question of his entire ministry. Who is the Son of Man? What
are people saying about him? Opinions were varied. Herod thought
that Jesus might be John the Baptizer come back from the grave. Some
wondered whether he was Elijah, prominent in Hebrew lore as the
prophet chosen to anoint the Messiah and lead Israel to repentance
and faith. Many had considered John to be Elijah returned from heav-
en (11:14). Jeremiah was believed by some of the more pious in Israel
to have ascended bodily into heaven as reward for his prophetic ministry on behalf of Israel.

Matthew succinctly records the heart of this crucial dialog. The Son of
Man is the Messiah, Son of the living God. He is not merely a prophet
or one of the outstanding prophets of Israel. He is the anointed Shepherd. All who confess him as Messiah and Son are blessed by God, a
blessing, which the messianic community surely enjoys. Human weakness can never comprehend this staggering truth. Faith that Jesus is the
Messiah is always revealed by his Father in heaven (6:9). The magnitude of this revelation becomes all the more apparent when the Father
in heaven reveals that Jesus executes a mission, which will lead him
through suffering and death to glorious resurrection (16:21).

The Messianic Community (Church) 16:18–28

The word, church (Hebrew: *qahal,* called ones, assembly; Greek: *ekklesia,* assembly), denotes the assembly, community or congregation of God's Covenant people. The very powers of death and all that is inimical to the messianic community shall never imprison or conquer those who are part of it. By revelation of the Father Simon (Aramaic: *Cephas*; Greek: *Petros,* rock-man) confesses that Jesus is Christ and Son of God. Upon such a foundation (Greek: *petra,* rock) the community stands. The notion was not new or radical. Hebrew tradition named Abraham the rock upon which God built the world. On New Testament thought, the spiritual community (church) is built upon the apostles and prophets, Jesus himself being the chief cornerstone (Ephesians 2:20). In the grand vision penned by Jesus' servant John, the twelve foundations of the heavenly city of God bear the names of the twelve apostles (Apocalypse 21:14). Within the city the writer sees no temple. For God and the Lamb are the Temple.

Keys are symbols of authority within the kingdom. To Jesus, the keys of death and hell have been given by virtue of his death and resurrection (Apocalypse 1:18; 3:7; cf. Isaiah 22:22). Keys are authority to teach in Yahweh's name (Matthew 23:9–13), a unique privilege and function exercised heretofore by Scribes and Pharisees. By this appointment, Peter (and all the apostles) becomes, as it were, chief rabbi in the new Israel with power to bind and loose. The divine authority, which had belonged to priests, elders and teachers of the Law (16:21) now belongs to the new community, which openly confesses God's Son as Messiah and Lord.

An overzealous interpretation of the position and role of the man Simon Peter is counteracted by the unusual and surprising incident, which follows. Peter is addressed as Satan. He is an offense to God. By his overly demonstrative and rash rebuke he shows that he's not on God's side at all (16:23). The community as a whole is "successor" to Peter. Unfortunately it can sometimes manifest unbecoming pride, inexcusable ignorance and tragic littleness of faith. Fortunately the community is securely built upon Christ himself whom, in Spirit-wrought faith, it confesses as Savior and Lord.

That the Son of the living God should terminate his earthly mission by suffering and dying was and remains a stumbling block. Those who imagine (or hope) that the Messiah's church must rival earthly powers and be vested with marks of pomp and glory easily take offense when the church undergoes persecution and hardship. But the real offense with which the church must contend is the proclamation of the cross, symbol of suffering and shame. Yet the church must not only boast in the cross, but actually glory in it. For through this message God offers salvation (cf. I Corinthians 1:18–24). Furthermore, the community must stand ready to bear its own crosses in the Messiah's name. Discipleship involves sacrifice and commitment.

Glory on the Mount 17:1–23

One facet of the rich lore of messianic expectation was the belief that God's righteous people would shine like the sun at the day of resurrection. The Transfiguration, in which the Messiah's face beams as brightly as the sun, prefigures his resurrection the third day after suffering death at the hands of the Sanhedrin (16:21; cf. Apocalypse 1:16). The locale is usually identified as Mt. Hermon. The glory of God resting upon his Messiah is witnessed by Peter, James and John. They will witness a far different scene, as well: his anguish and sorrow in Gethsemane (26:37). Moses and Elijah, symbols of the Law and Prophets, both received mountaintop revelations from God (Exodus 24:15–18; I Kings 19:8–18). Reference to booths is clearly understood by Jewish readers in the context of Tabernacles. The seventh day of the feast was identified with messianic hopes (Leviticus 23:27–43).

The testimony Jesus received at his baptism (3:13–17) is repeated. The solemn injunction to heed the words of Jesus reminds readers at once of the predictive words attributed to Moses (Deuteronomy 18:15; cf. Acts 3:22–23). Mountaintop experiences give way to the reality of a world in which their Messiah must suffer and die. Their question regarding Elijah and restoration elicits the reminder that Jesus identified John as Elijah (11:14) in fulfillment of Malachi 4:5. Old Israel did not recognize or receive his preparatory message of repentance. Neither does it recognize or receive Jesus as the Messiah. He will experience the same rejection and fate accorded John. There is one staggering difference: Jesus will rise from the dead.

Healing the epileptic is described in terms strongly reminiscent of a former miracle (8:13).

Those called by Jesus to continue his mission and ministry were unable to effect the healing because of their weakness and littleness of faith, something, which they had sadly demonstrated prior to this recorded episode (14:16; 26; 15:23,33; 16:22). At the moment they represent a faithless and perverse generation, which virtually has no faith at all. Even the tiniest grain of genuine, trusting faith would enable them to "move mountains," a proverbial saying for overcoming the greatest of obstacles (Isaiah 40:4; 54:10). When Jesus speaks of his approaching rejection and condemnation, they are greatly distressed. They understand neither the meaning of his death nor the significance of his promised resurrection. Even after witnessing diving glory on the mount, they fail fully to comprehend what the community could only grasp after the outpouring of the Holy Spirit on Pentecost.

Discussion

1. Why is Herod a classic example of a tormented conscience? Are "pangs of conscience" always detrimental to spiritual and emotional health?

2. Why is it important for Christians today to hold that Jesus is Lord over all traditions? To what can traditions, even wholesome and helpful ones, sometimes lead?

3. Why is religion susceptible to hypocrisy?

4. Upon what (or whom) is the church really built? How does the word "church" define one facet of what it really is?

5. What is Matthew simply and clearly witnessing about Jesus to his primarily Jewish readers/hearers?

CHAPTER TEN

Life in the Kingdom
Matthew 17:24–20:28

By recording a series of discourses Jesus held with his disciples, Matthew sharply delineates life and discipline within the community, which confesses Jesus to be the Messiah and Son of the living God. Matthew selects sayings (logia) which relate to political and societal obligations; greatness in the kingdom; the matter of offense; relationships between members of the community of faith relative to sin and forgiveness; marriage and divorce; children and their place in the community; attitudes toward temporal possessions and wealth; service and suffering on the part of the people of God. Matthew also weaves into this segment of his narrative an additional prediction of the suffering, death and resurrection of the Son of Man.

A clearly established thematic connection with the preceding section of this Gospel is discerned. Jesus speaks of the Church (16:18; 18:17). He deals with Peter (16:16–18; 22–23; 17:24–25; 18:21). He widens the binding and loosing authority to include the entire community represented by the disciples (16:19; 18:18). He discusses in considerable details the nature of faith (17:16–21; 18:1–14). This new segment actually begins with 17:24, not 18:1. It must be remembered that chapter and verse divisions have been added to the text purely for the sake of convenience and easy reference. They are totally absent from earliest manuscripts.

Freedom 17:24–27

Pharisees were ready to forge strange, even unnatural alliances to attain their own religious and political goals. Herodians were sympathetic to the otherwise despised and hated Roman government. Both groups seek to ensnare Jesus in a blatantly political trap. The sensitive issue is payment of taxes to Caesar (22:17). They pose a similar question regarding payment of the Temple tax. A half-shekel (Greek: didrachma) was levied on every male Jew above the age of nineteen. It was used to maintain Temple worship (Exodus 30:11ff). After destruction of the Temple by the Roman army (A.D. 70), Jews were forced to pay the tax to support a hated pagan shrine dedicated to Jupiter. The Greek stater equaled one shekel, payment for two persons.

Jesus deftly fends off the potentiality incendiary query. Families of earthly monarchs are usually free, i.e., exempt from royal taxation. Disciples of the Messiah are family of the King of heaven. They too are free. Nevertheless, Jesus and his disciples willingly submit to the Mosaic requirement, just as they render Caesar things due human government (22:21). Freedom in Christ is never to be construed as either free-for-all or free-from-all. Life in the Messiah's kingdom entails responsibility and discipline. Christians recognized their legal obligations as citizens of the temporal realm, themes discussed by St. Paul in Romans 13:1–7 (cf. I Peter 2:13–17).

Greatness in the Kingdom 18:1–6

Rank in the Jewish community was highly structured. Scribes, elders and chief priests constituted the Sanhedrin, supreme council of Judaism (16:21). After the close of the so-called Babylonian exile (538 B.C.), Pharisees assumed the role of official custodians of Torah. Scribes and Pharisees sat in Moses' seat. This symbolized their authority to interpret the Mosaic codes, transmit tradition, legislate binding rules of faith and conduct and grant exemptions from them (16:19). There is little question that they were considered greatest in the kingdom of God on earth.

Placing a small child in the midst of the disciples, Jesus cautions that if they do not become as little children they will not even enter the kingdom. Jesus stresses not only humility; one must show childlike trust toward the grace of God. Christian faith is utter and total dependence. The child of the Father in heaven has nothing looks to God for all. In the Messianic community, whoever receives a childlike believer in the name of Christ receives Christ himself. Whoever scandalizes a child of God offends Christ. Greatness in his community is never measured in terms of rank or position; it is commensurate with the degree of trust one has in the promises and mercies of God.

Concern for the Community 18:6–14

Offenses cause believers to fall away from their faith. The word (Greek: *scandalon*, scandal, stumbling block) is found elsewhere in Matthew's Gospel (5:29–30; 11:6; 15:12; 16:23; 17:27; 24:10; 26:33). Such offenses are actually committed against the Messiah. His people must never be instruments or channels through which temptations to sin come. References to bodily parts may be metaphorical allusions to the church as the body of Christ. This theme is skillfully developed in considerable detail in Epistles of Paul (I Corinthians 12; Romans 12), but it is not at all certain if that is the intended meaning here. At any rate, the Messianic community must cut off from the new Israel those who persistently offend and scandalize it.

Childlike (not childish) believers must neither be despised nor held in disdain. Quite the contrary! They enjoy relationship with beings of exceptionally high rank. Angels have direct access to the Father in heaven. Rivalries and jealousies break fraternal bonds of peace. The community is to reach out in loving concern for all who might stray from it as sheep wander away from the flock (24:4–5). This reflects the compassion of the Shepherd who seeks out his flock when some of the sheep are scattered abroad (Ezekiel 34:12).

Sin and Forgiveness 18:15–35

God is perfect (5:48). Believers strive for perfection in life and conduct when fail. Repentance is thus a daily spiritual exercise. When a member sins or offends, the spiritual family reasons with the offender in strict privacy (cf. Leviticus 19:17f). If this fails to produce reconciliation, the assembly must finally act. One who refuses to listen to the corrective voice of the Church (16:18) is separated from the fellowship. Authority to bind and loose come from the Messiah. As the Church acts, he acts. In Judaism, ten males were required in order to have corporate worship. The Messiah is in the midst of his community when only two or three gather in his name (18:20).

Jewish tradition stipulated that one offer pardon to the offender at least four times. Peter suggests a possible seven-fold ministration of forgiveness. Jesus raised it to seventy times seven as he minds the disciples of Genesis 4:24. Revenge is to be replaced by unlimited forgiveness. Ten thousand talents represent over one billion dollars. One hundred denarii represent something like twenty or twenty-five dollars. While compassion rules in the kingdom, obstinately offending and unforgiving members are finally removed (18:17f). Those who refuse to forgive (18:22) forfeit God's forgiveness.

Marriage, Divorce and Children 19:1–15

Jesus leaves Galilee for Judea to resume his healing ministry. He attracts large crowds. In this context, Jesus disputes with certain Pharisees regarding marriage and divorce. Matthew has already recorded a logion regarding certificates of divorce (5:31f). The question at issue here deals with sufficient grounds for divorce. While allowances granted by Moses were more concession than permission, Jesus does recognize that adultery dissolves the marriage vow. Eunuchs were labeled outcasts (Deuteronomy 23:1). In Judaism an unmarried rabbi was an oddity. Both marriage and celibacy are mysteries, which Jesus neither commands nor forbids. While asceticism was practiced by a number of religious sects, including the one at Qumran, marriage continues to be a part of God's good creation. In must not be forbidden. It is in the world or age to come that men and women will not be given in marriage (22:30).

It was a popular custom to seek a blessing for children. On the great Day of Atonement, parents frequently sought this. The kingdom, as Jesus previously pointed out, belongs to children since they depend on the grace of God without demand or reservation. The Christian community came to see in the words of Jesus a reference to baptism of children. In their original context, no baptismal allusion is evident. The phrase, do not hinder them, appears in connection with Jesus' own baptism (3:14), the baptism of the Ethiopian eunuch (Acts 8:36) and the baptism of Gentile converts (Acts 10:47; 11:17).

Possessions 19:16–24

This discourse is prompted by the third of five questions recorded in Matthew. All are addressed to Jesus. The first is proffered by Pharisees (19:3), the second by his own disciples (19:10) and the third by a wealthy, young man (19:16–22). This, in turn, elicits a fourth (19:25), followed by the fifth question posed by Peter (19:27).

The young man is concerned about a lifestyle, which will guarantee him life in the age to come. God, who alone is good, reveals his will in the Law. Jesus recites commandments, which comprise the so-called second table of the Law, which deal with interpersonal relationships. Their summary is expressed is Leviticus 19:18. Jesus will repeat it in a different context (22:34–40). Jesus does not dispute the man's claim of obedience. Neither does he add a rule or command, which will automatically assure perfection. Life in the kingdom of God summons one to put God first one's trust, loyalties and commitments (6:24–34). Undue concern for temporal possessions may constitute a block to discipleship. The obviously sincere young man may think that he was observing what Jesus later calls the second great commandment (22:38f). In reality, he failed to love and trust in God above all else. Furthermore, salvation is quite beyond the power and ability of any human being. To save oneself by one's own deeds is as impossible as the passage of a camel through the eye of a needle. Salvation and eternal life with God are totally a gift of his grace

The Good and Gracious Will of God 19:25–20:28

In the regeneration, i.e., the new age ushered in when the Son of Man comes in glory to execute judgment (25:31–46), the apostles of the Messiah will share his rule over new Israel. Each who sacrifices in order to confess Jesus as Lord will receive many times that willingly given. Each disciple will inherit that life, which the young, rich man was earnestly seeking. Many in this present age who seem to be among the first will be the last. In the age to come, the poor in spirit who seek first the kingdom of God will be first. An inheritance is a gift. God's good and gracious will is extended to the last up to the first (20:8) of those whom he calls. Rewards for service and sacrifice in the Messiah's name are rewards of grace, not human merit.

Jesus sets out upon his final journey to Jerusalem. Matthew has recorded previous predictions of Jesus' passion and death. Mocking, scourging and death by crucifixion are here mentioned for the first time. Crucifixion was decidedly not a Jewish practice. It would be carried out by Gentiles, i.e., by the Roman government. Jesus again makes it clear that true greatness in this present age does not depend on rank or authority; it depends on service. Among pagans, greatness is measured in terms of power. Rome will demonstrate that kind of power as it sentences the very Messiah of God to death. But Jesus drinks the cup of judgment and death as an example for the apostles. He did not come to be served, but to serve and give his life as an offering and ransom for sin (20:28). As Son of God, he could have demanded that he be served. Satan even offered him all the kingdoms, power and glory, which the world has to offer (4:9). Jesus refused them. He came as the devoted servant of Yahweh (Isaiah 53:11f). He will suffer and die as substitute for sinners.

Discussion

1. What do "church" and "kingdom of God" have in common? What does each term stress when applied to the people of God?

2. How does our Lord deftly define Christian freedom? Is freedom in Christ to be understood as a free-for-all? How does St. Paul treat this issue in Romans 6 and Galatians 5:16–25?

3. Does Jesus teach us that faith must be childish to be genuine?

4. Why can the English word "offense (or offended)" be easily misunderstood when used with reference to 18:6–14?

CHAPTER ELEVEN

David's Son is David's Lord
Matthew 20:29–22:46

The Son of Man is to be condemned by the religious leaders of Israel and delivered to the secular authorities. Matthew sketches the final episode in the Messiah's healing ministry prior to that deliverance. He restores sight to blind beggars. This act foreshadows the spiritual restoration achieved by Jesus' suffering, death and resurrection. Opening the eyes of the blind (11:2–6) is another sign of the Messianic age (Isaiah 29:18; 35:5). Matthew is keenly aware of that. He intends to stress the conviction that this age has been inaugurated in the ministry of Jesus the Messiah. The blind suppliants address Jesus as Son of David. Each Davidic king was considered an adopted son of Yahweh, anointed to rule as God's agent. Jesus is the true Son of David, hence the true King of Israel, because he is the true Son of God.

Behold Your King 21:1–22

Jesus' entry into the royal city is seen as fulfillment of the ancient prophecy recorded in Zechariah 9:9. He deliberately goes to the Mount of Olives, known among Jews as the site of messianic judgment (Zechariah 14:4). Multitudes accord Jesus a reception similar to festive celebrations associated with the Feast of Tabernacles, also reminiscent of 2 Kings 9:13. Jesus is greeted with the ancient prayer, Hosanna (Hebrew: save, help) (Psalm 118:25f; 2 Kings 6:26). Crowds hail him with fervor and enthusiasm as they ask Yahweh to bless him who has come as prophet (21:11), priest (20:28) and king (21:5).

The Messiah exercises this threefold role (or office) in cleansing the Temple. Legitimate currency exchange was quite permissible. Greek and Roman coins would and could be easily traded to provide the half-shekel with which the tax was paid (17:24–27). The holiest shrine of Israel had been desecrated by abuse. Purification of the Temple is also a mark of the messianic age.

Matthew's witness to the mission of the Messiah is drawing to a close.
Jesus' citation of words from Isaiah 56:7 and Jeremiah 7:11 stress his
authority in fulfillment of Malachi 3:1ff. The Temple incident and
healings which follow serve as unmistakable testimony that the Son of
David has come to his people. He who is greater than Moses, Sabbath,
priests and Temple is in their midst (12:1–8). Children see what their
leaders fail to perceive. In striking contrast, they acclaim Jesus who receives their confession in light of Psalm 8:3.

Cursing of the fig tree is symbolic of judgment (3:7–10). Israel has
failed to bear fruits of faith and obedience. But his disciples' own
faith is subject to weakness and doubt (17:20). It is only as they trust
in the grace of God and bear fruits of love that they will escape similar judgment. The divine partner has ever right to expect fruits from
his people.

Controversy and Challenge 21:23–22:40

Matthew records five significant controversies involving Jesus and
the religious authorities of Israel. Each follows the pattern of instruction widely employed by rabbis. Each question represents a different
segment of Judaism. Chief priests and elders challenge Jesus' right to
teach. Pharisees and Herodians seek to ensnare him in a political trap.
Sadducees question his theology of resurrection. Scribes challenge his
understanding of the Torah. These discussions are preliminary to a final question asked by Jesus regarding God's Messiah.

By What Authority? 21:23–22:14

Matthew situates the first great controversy in one of the porticos near
the court of Gentiles. Chief priests and elders challenge Jesus for assuming authority in their Temple. Authority was a neuralgic concern
of those who claimed exclusive rights in Israel. Does Jesus claim divine
authority or does he presume his own competence to sufficient? Rabbinical methodology often took the form of counter-question. What
authority lay behind the baptism of John who had sorely rebuked both
Pharisees and Sadducees? John's ministry was to prepare the way of the
Lord (3:7–12). Jesus' authority is similar to that of John.

The parables sharpen the clear contrast between Jesus' authority and

the incompetence of those who are challenging him. They teach Torah; but they do not repent. They claim to be stewards of God's vineyard; but they reject the owner's son. They insist they are the true servants and prophets of Yahweh; they turn form THE prophet whose
interpretation of Psalm 118:22f reveals that Israel's Messiah is the cornerstone of the Church. Jesus pointedly castigates their arrogant, self-
satisfying pride. A patient Yahweh requires of his people faithfulness,
love and obedience. Those called into his kingdom must bear fruits of
repentance and faith and be clothed with wedding garments of holi-
ness, which exceeds that claimed by Scribes and Pharisees (5:20).

Is It Lawful? 22:15–22

The second great controversy centers on a crucial point of interpretation. Does Torah allow payment of taxes to a pagan power, in this
instance, the Roman emperor? Pharisees opposed the practice because
it signified political subjugation. Herodians generally supported it because their king (tetrarch) was a puppet of Rome. The ill-matched delegation, which seeks to ensnare him in a neat trap addresses Jesus with
feigned deference. He teaches the way of God, a technical phrase for
instruction later adopted by the messianic community (Acts 9:2). An
affirmative reply on the part of Jesus will estrange him from the people.
A negative reply will constitute cause for civil action against him. Jesus
replies with true rabbinic skill. The principle of civil authority does
not clash with life in the kingdom (cf. 17:24–27).

Whose Wife Will She Be? 22:23–33

The third controversy deals with resurrection of the body, a doctrine
popularly taught by Pharisees, but rejected by Sadducees. The problem
posed is merely a pretext. But it refers to a custom described in Deuteronomy 25:5–6. Sadducees attempt to demonstrate the utter absurdity
of a teaching, which they claim could not be found in Torah. Jesus
reveals their ignorance, both of the Scriptures and the power of God.
In resurrection existence, God's people are like angels in that there
are no sexual relationships. This is a particularly compelling response
since Sadducees also rejected the doctrine of angels. As for the teaching itself, Jesus finds the reality of resurrection in his understanding of
Exodus 3:6–16. Yahweh is God of the patriarchs. In this point of time

they have already experienced physical death. Yet, to Jesus' mind, God regards them as virtually alive in view of the resurrection of the dead.

Which is the Great Commandment? 22:24–40

The fourth controversy tests Jesus' understanding of what for Jews was the very core of Torah. They tended to give equal weight and importance to all requirements of the Decalog. At the same time, they regarded love for God and one's neighbor to be the epitome of Torah. They are apparently testing Jesus' attitude toward a generally accepted theological tenet.

Deuteronomy 6:5 constitutes part of the creed of Israel. In Hebrew psychology, heart, soul and mind form the totality of the individual. The great commandment is that one must love God with one's entire being. The Greek text (Septuagint) of Leviticus 19:18 understands neighbor as a fellow human being in Israel. These two great commandments bespeak the essence of God's holy will toward his people.

Jesus' attitude toward Torah and its divine authority over the people of God radically distinguishes him form current leaders of Judaism. Matthew has recorded a number of remarkable reinterpretations. The Messianic community is to show love for enemies (5:43). One is to do toward others as one would wish others to do to oneself (7:12). Love and mercy always takes precedence over Sabbath rules (12:1–14). Moreover, in the final judgment, love is that which the Son of Man commends (25:31–40). Love is the unfailing fruit of faith. It exceeds all attempts at humanly devised efforts to achieve righteousness (5:20).

What Do You Think of the Messiah? 22:41–46

Jesus defines the final area of controversy. He challenges Pharisees to reexamine their position as to Davidic descent of the Messiah. That the Messiah should issue from the stem and family of David was a widely held belief (Isaiah 11:1; Jeremiah 23:5). The thrust of Jesus' question goes far deeper than mere surface belief. How does David, prompted by the Holy Spirit, call Messiah his Lord? Every king in Israel was considered a son of David and, in an adoptive sense, a son of Yahweh. But David never calls every royal descendent his Lord. Only the Messiah is, at the same time, David's son and Lord. This answers the paradox. It also provides another clear and telling witness to the faith of the early Christian community of believers. In acknowledging and confessing Jesus as heir to the royal Davidic throne, it reechoed the bold confession made by the incipient messianic community: Jesus is the Messiah, the Son of the living God.

Discussion

1. Of what is the healing of the blind both sign and symbol? Why is the title "Son of David" rightly applied to Jesus even though he was considered to be a legal son of Joseph (1:16)?

2. What is the precise meaning of "Hosanna" in the Palm Sunday greeting?

3. Which Jewish sect at the time of Jesus confessed belief in a resurrection? Which one denied it?

4. What is a brief, yet complete, summation of the law of God?

Conclusion

In this rather lengthy segment of his Gospel, Matthew has incorporated significant instances of healings and other wonder-works, which stress the authority and mission of the Messiah. The crucial event, which as no other demonstrates Jesus' authority, is that in which he links restoration to physical wholeness with restoration to spiritual wholeness. The totally unexpected pronouncement of forgiveness of sin elicited from the startled multitudes a religious fervor, which glorified God for bestowing such power on earth. That authority is again exercised when Jesus enlists the Twelve in his mission and commits to them power to proclaim the kingdom, cast out demons, heal all kinds of disease, cleanse lepers and even raise the dead. Messianic teaching authority is highlighted as well as Matthew relates so many perceptive parables of the kingdom, discourses of Jesus regarding life in the kingdom and controversies in which Jesus is engaged with his detractors.

Source of authority for his God-given mission is abundantly evident from the episodes, which occurred at Caesarea Philippi and the mount on which Jesus was gloriously transfigured. Jesus is not only confessed by divined revelation as Son of the living God; he is endorsed as Messiah and Prophet by the appearance of Moses and Elijah. He is indeed to be deemed greater than all that was so highly prized and treasured by the people of God. He is greater than Moses, Jonah, Solomon, Sabbath, Temple, priests, Israel, tradition, even Torah itself, as whose fulfillment and final interpreter he appeared.

People recognized the authority, which enables him to perform his mission, even while their leaders remained obstinately blind to it. Opposition to both his authority and mission increased in intensity and finally led to over attempts to silence him permanently.

Part Three

Passion and Commission of the Messiah

$$+|+$$
$$+|+$$

Matthew records additional discourses of Jesus in which he addresses both multitudes who are following him and disciples whom he has selected to carry on his mission and ministry in the Messiah's name. Discourses selected provide a fitting conclusion to the mission and authority of Jesus so carefully reviews by the author. They also link the Messiah's ministry and the growing enmity on the part of religious leaders engendered by it, to his suffering, death and resurrection. It is more than coincidental that Matthew arranges the discourses so that Jesus concludes them by speaking to his disciples alone (24:1–25:46).

The discourses contain seven severe and solemn condemnations, a tragic lament over the city of Jerusalem, signs and warnings regarding the end-time and seven parables, which deal with the return (parousia) of the Son of Man with unquestioned authority to execute judgment. Matthew then provides a precise and detailed record of what has come to be termed the passion of our Lord. True to his purpose and methodology, Matthew sees various incidents of the passion as occurring within the context of fulfillment (26:54–56). He brings his dynamic witness – and that of the early Christian community – to a triumphal close by proclaiming the resurrection and enthronement of God's Messiah, along with the royal commission to make disciples of all nations.

The first pronouncements deal with apostasy. Matthew understands apostasy in terms of rejection. At the birth of God's Anointed One, Jerusalem fails to receive him. Herod seeks to destroy him. Leaders of Israel establish a pattern of rejection as they repudiate the preparatory ministry of John. They condemn Jesus for pursuing fellowship with those whom they have labeled societal outcasts. They repeatedly seek to entrap him in his teaching. They accuse him of complicity with Satan. They ignore his testimony and twist his own witness to his person and mission. They charge him with blasphemy. They unjustly sentence him to death. They hand him over to Gentiles for judgment. They are an evil and apostate generation (12:39). Their house is left desolate (23:38).

CHAPTER TWELVE

Apostasy of Israel
Matthew 23:1–36

Condemnation and Warning 23:1–36

Controversy reaches climactic heights as the Messiah denounces both Scribes and Pharisees for blatant deceit and hypocrisy. They sit in Moses' seat, symbolic reference to their authority to instruct the people. Often an actual stone was placed in front of the synagogue from which they delivered their legal interpretations. People are to pay heed to them when their teachings are in accord with Mosaic Law. But the leaders fail to practice what they teach. Rules and regulations formulated in their traditions (Halakoth) were a burdensome yoke, from which they were free to exempt themselves. Phylacteries were small leather cases attached to the head and left arm in accordance with Deuteronomy 6:8; 11:13–22. They contained selected verses of Scripture. Pious Jews also wore tassels on their outer garments. Jesus himself may have worn such (9:20). Pharisees usually made their tassels long and their leather cases broad to accentuate their devotion and piety.

The respected title, Rabbi, was deferentially accorded a recognized teacher of Torah. Though Jesus was given the title (22:16; 24; 36; 26:25, 49), he admonishes his disciples to eschew all titles since they have but one Rabbi and Father in heaven. Leaders in the community founded by the Messiah are to avoid vanity and ostentatious salutations lest they succumb to pride and hypocrisy. Matthew has already recorded the logion, which equates greatness in the kingdom with service (20:25–28).

Matthew records seven searing condemnations:

1. By their hypocrisy and false teaching, Scribes and Pharisees close the kingdom to those who follow them (23:13).
2. Proselytes, i.e., Gentiles who embrace the full ritual and beliefs of Judaism can easily imbibe a spirit of self-righteousness, which

always leads one away from the saving mercies of God (23:15).

3. Swearing (not cursing), i.e., binding oneself to an oath in God's name was not to be broken. Scribes and Pharisees permitted the breaking of a vow if it were by less holy things. Jesus disavows this as pure legalese, invoked solely to circumvent the nature of an oath (23:16–22). Jesus had already instructed his own disciples that a simple yes or no suffices (5:33–37). Once again Messiah's enemies reveal their spiritual blindness.

4. Tithing of mint, dill and cumin are not prescribed by Moses. Scribes demanded it as part of their interpretation. Such is allowable if it stems from proper spiritual motives. But justice, mercy and faithfulness to the will of God must not be thereby neglected. Energies can be expended on gnat-like matters of religion while love is ignored (23:23f).

5. How easily religious practices can degenerate to external form! Undue concern about ritual purification can lead one to forget that the heart must be in the right relationship with God (23:25f; cf. 15:11–20).

6. Sepulchers were whitewashed to protect people from unwitting contact with a grave. Tombs are full of death and decay. Outward religious zeal can be little more than pious covering of spiritual decay and death (23:20). Small wonder the Messiah expects from his followers righteousness, which exceeds that of Scribes and Pharisees (5:20).

7. Herod the Great had erected a monument at the grave of David. Monuments to righteous martyrs stood as tokens of respect, even veneration. They were frequently decorated. When these spiritual leaders boast that they would never have participated in the martyrdom of God's honored prophets, Jesus charges them with witnessing against themselves. They are sons of those who did murder the prophets. Moreover, they will kill the last and greatest prophet of all (21:38f). They will persecute to the death those commissioned to proclaim his word (10:16–23). Persecution will, in fact, be so severe and ruthless that all the innocent blood shed from the time of Abel to Zachariah will be upon them! Historian Josephus refers to a certain Zachariah, son of Baruch, who was martyred in the Temple prior to the destruction of Jerusalem (23:29–36).

By means of this predictive oracle, Jesus concludes his condemnation of those who sit in Moses' seat of authority. It introduces his lament over the city and his prediction of its destruction and the end of the age. The apostasy of Israel, represented by its leaders, is complete. Tenants of God's vineyard beat, stoned and murdered the prophets whom God sent to it. They are about to kill the son and heir. God's vineyard will be given to new tenants (21:33–41).

O Jerusalem, Jerusalem 23:37–39

The Messiah weeps and laments over Zion, city of God whose magnificent Temple stood as symbol of Yahweh's presence with his people. Speaking with full messianic authority, Jesus reminds his hearers that he willed to gather Jerusalem's children together under his protective care. They chose not to be gathered. The consequence is truly horrendous. They are forsaken. With that somber pronouncement, Jesus concludes his woes on the leaders of Israel. The words have a truly ominous ring. The glory of Israel has departed from the Temple of Israel. Judgment has begun.

Discussion

1. Why could Jesus properly be addressed as "Rabbi" when the majority of his people rejected him?

2. Which contemporary religious practices can easily become meaningless external forms? Does repetition foster externalism? Must it?

3. How are we to understand our Lord's laments, condemnations, and warnings? Was there hope for the people who heard them? What is the role of repentance?

CHAPTER THIRTEEN

End of the Age
Matthew 24–25

Matthew's account of Jesus' scathing condemnations is followed by his recording the great eschatological (Greek: eschaton, last, final; relating to last things) discourse of Jesus with his disciples. It bears the literary characteristics of a valedictory. Judgment such as that spoken over Scribes and Pharisees has been a prominent them in this Gospel. The theme culminates in the highly dramatic scene, which is dominated by the return of the Son of Man. He comes in glory to announce the Father's decree (25:46).

This segment of Matthew's narrative is generally thought to be apocalyptic in form and structure. Apocalyptic (Greek: revelational, uncovering that which is hidden) literature consists of revelational or predictive material colored by the liberal use of highly symbolic numbers, names and events, cosmological cataclysms, the prominent role of angels (and demons) and themes of divine victory and retribution. A good deal of apocalyptic literature is found in portions of Isaiah, Ezekiel and Daniel. A rich body of such writings developed as well during the so-called intertestamental period.

Jesus speaks of three quite remarkable and truly momentous events. They are spiritually related, but historically distinct:

1. Destruction of the Temple
2. Return of the Messiah
3. End of the age

Once again, Jesus speaks with that authority, which is his as Son of God and Messiah.

Predictions and Catastrophe 24:1–31
Various structures constituted the refurbished sacred complex, which had been a pet project of Herod the Great. He undertook the costly

renovation some forty-six years before as an enduring monument to his reign. The disciples focus particularly on the Temple, the very heart of Hebrew cults and worship. The Temple, with its elaborate ceremonies and daily sacrifices, will pass away. Every stone will be thrown down. This occurred when both the city and Temple were utterly destroyed after a prolonged siege by Roman armies A.D. 66–70. Matthew depicts Jesus sitting on the Mount of Olives overlooking the city. The scene itself is strongly suggestive of Ezekiel 8–11 in which the prophet sketches the glory of God departing from the Temple of God. The disciples pose three direct and probing questions: When will the destruction of the Temple occur? What is the sign of Jesus' return? What is the sign of the consummation of the age?

Jesus does not rebuke or turn aside their curiosity as unwarranted speculation. He uses their questions to warn against deception. False messiahs and false prophets will appear. They will succeed in leading many of the messianic community astray by means of great signs and wonders, which they will perform. They will claim to know exactly where the Messiah is exactly when he will return. Unfortunately, some will always be ready to listen to them even though Jesus clearly declares that only the Father has that information.

There are certain signs, which specifically point to the end of the age (24:4–14). Wars, suffering, tribulation and natural disasters are potent reminders of the Lord's promise. Yet not every conflict or famine or catastrophe or seemingly unnatural cosmic event is a sure sign that the end is imminent. They are to be viewed as birth pangs of travail, which is to come. The appearance of false messiahs and prophets, wars and natural upheavals are a prelude to great tribulation. Members of Jesus' community will be persecuted and hated simply because they confess him as Messiah and Savior. The community itself will sadly experience apostasy, marked by betrayal, hatred and false teaching. Those who stand fast in their confession will be saved. Furthermore, the good news of the kingdom will be shared in spite of uncertainty with regard to things to come.

Jesus' allusion to the desolating sacrilege of the holy place is described in Daniel 9:27; 11:31; 12:1. Antiochus Epiphanes, vain ruler of Syria, erected in the very heart of the Temple an altar to his own veneration (168 B.C.). This was so repugnant to Jews that it triggered the Maccabean revolt, which permitted Israel a few years of political freedom. This historical act of profaning the Temple lay behind much of the political turmoil and religious tension, which existed between Jerusalem and Rome. The practice of raising the imperial eagle over conquered territories infuriated Jews who considered such an act idolatrous and blasphemous. Sedition and rebellion were commonplace. In retaliation, Caligula (A.D. 40) threatened to duplicate the act of Antiochus.

Jesus directs that when the desolating sacrilege occurs (Rome destroyed both city and Temple A.D. 70), those in Judea should flee. Sabbath restrictions would still be in effect for Jews. When the siege of Jerusalem became apparent, the messianic community fled to Pella in northern Perea. It was, in fact, for the sake of the community that the time and tribulation of those events should be shortened. Jewish Christians might surmise that Jesus' would return immediately after the desecration of the Temple. It is but one sign of Jesus' return with great power and glory. As signs do unfold, some will always be eager to claim they have inside or privileged information, which others do not possess. The Lord will return. Signs will find fulfillment. But it has not been revealed to anyone, prophet or inner circle of enlightened initiates, exactly when that will happen. Excessive and extravagant claims of exact information are to be adjudged false prophecy.

When the ensign of the Son of Man does appear, tribes of the earth will mourn as they behold the glory of the Messiah whom they have spurned (Zechariah 12). The trumpet will sound (Isaiah 27:13) as the Son of Man gathers his believers from out of the world at the end of the age (Daniel 7:13).

Preparations for the Messiah's Return 24:32–46
Jesus concludes his eschatological discourse with seven parables, though his description of final judgment is probably to be classified as an eschatological vision. Purpose is to encourage members of the community, which confesses him as Lord to endurance (24:13), watchful preparation (24:42) and faithful stewardship during the waiting period.

1. The fig tree. God's people must neither grow impatient at his delay nor careless with regard to responsible watchfulness. Signs will be fulfilled in the Father's own time. The words, nor the Son, are absent

from some manuscripts of Matthew's Gospel but are undoubtedly genuine (24:36). Understanding human proclivity to religious self-aggrandizement, Jesus stresses that no private revelations, ecstatic visions or special knowledge of the Messiah's exact return will be given. Speculation is absolutely futile and dangerous. The Father in heaven initiates and completes his mission in his Messiah in his time, according to his will. A fig tree also suggests summer harvest with its symbolic reference to ingathering (24:22,31).

2. Days of Noah. God's people can become so preoccupied with daily matters (which in and of themselves may not at all be sinful) that they fail to watch. The flood finally came in accordance with the word of Noah. The end of the age will finally come in accord with the word of Jesus (24:35).

3. The household. The coming of the Messiah will be as unexpected as the approach of a burglar. Jesus will return at an hour none expects. Each house must watch and pray!

4. Faithful servants. As they watch and pray, God's people are occupied with God's work. Unfaithful servants, possibly an allusion to leaders within the messianic community, are neither watching nor praying nor serving. They will be separated from the faithful and joined to those who rejected the Lord's salvation (24:43–51).

5. Bridesmaids. The community eagerly awaits and anticipates the arrival of Jesus, the Bridegroom. Rejection of the foolish maidens and closing of the door represent final judgment. Constant, unfailing watchfulness is called for since the precise day and hour are unknown (24:36; 42; 44; 50).

6. Responsible stewardship. Faith in the grace of God revealed in the life, death and resurrection of Christ shows itself in faithful use of God's gifts. Talents (originally measures of weight) were valued by the metal chosen for coinage. Silver talents were mans of easy exchange. Gifts from God are to be invested in the Messiah's work. Failure to employ gifts and abilities in a responsible manner demonstrates lack of faith and carelessness with regard to the Lord's return (25:14–30).

7. Last judgment. The narrative concludes the eschatological discourse. It is variously named parable of the shepherd or parable of sheep and goats (25:31–46). The criterion according to which

judgment is pronounced on all nations is not knowledge, zeal, fame, piety or even external membership in the community. It is love, manifested in works of the second great commandment, which naturally flow from the first great commandment of God's holy will (22:36–40). Loving response on the part of the faithful and wise servants who prayerfully watch for the Messiah's return constitutes righteousness, which exceeds that of Scribes and Pharisees (5:20). Such love serves the least of the needy with whom Jesus identifies himself. Such servants who in the Messiah's name exercise this love are blessed by the Father as they inherit the kingdom prepared from the foundation of the world.

Discussion

1. What is apocalyptic literature? Why does it always seem to be popular?
2. Is there such a thing as a "rapture" taught in 24:40?
3. Can anyone really predict an exact time for the return of Jesus?
4. What will false prophets and false messiahs be able to do? How can God's people check them out?
5. What is responsible Christian stewardship?

CHAPTER FOURTEEN

Passion of the Messiah
Matthew 26–27

Matthew carefully crafts his account of the Passion (condemnation and crucifixion) of the Messiah as he continues to focus his eye upon the twin themes of fulfillment and deliverance. He has already alluded to Jesus' sufferings, death and resurrection. Jonah was in the belly of the fish; the Son of Man will be in the heart of the earth (12:40). John's death prefigures the death of another of Yahweh's prophets (14:5; 23:31f). Jesus' own words regarding his impending fate are cited (16:21; 17:12, 22; 20:18f). Apostate tenants kill the son of the own of the vineyard (21:33–39).

Several incidents are now related, which clearly enunciate the themes. The entire narrative is set within the context of Passover (26:2–4), the great feast of commemoration of deliverance from bondage. The Passion occurs in accordance with Yahweh's gracious design, to which Jesus willingly submits (26:42) as one who came to serve and offer his life as ransom for sin (20:28). Anointing prepares Jesus for burial (26:12). Jesus fully realizes that his time is at hand (26:18). He will experience shameful betrayal by one of his own disciples (26:21–24). His blood will be poured out (26:28). He will be deserted and forsaken as the Shepherd of the flock is smitten (26:31). He is seized in Gethsemane to that the Scriptures might be fulfilled (26:54–56). False witnesses are sought to testify against him (26:59; cf. Psalm 35:11). He testifies under solemn oath that the Son of Man will be seated at the right hand of God and come in clouds of heaven (26:64; Daniel 7:13f).

Anointing and Betrayal 26:1–25

Passover links old and new covenants (testaments) of promise. In this instance it sets off a chain of events, which leads from commemoration and remembrance of God's unique deliverance of his people to sinister betrayal by a friend, to cruel crucifixion, to resurrection and enthronement. References to enemies assembled against God's Anointed are strongly suggestive of Psalm 2:2 (26:57–59; 27:1; 28:12).

Bethany lies east of the Mount of Olives. Anointing such as that experienced by Jesus was not uncommon in that culture. Jesus' disciples
claim to deplore what they considered a terrible waste of money. It
could better have been used for alms (6:2–4). In striking contrast, Jesus
praises the act of the woman as a beautiful work of love. This outpouring of love is superior to alms giving as it was usually practiced in that
day. Her act is more urgent at the moment because it is a powerfully
symbolic act. It constitutes pre-burial anointing of his body. Her faith
and love will be remembered (25:40). Reference to the whole world
serves as a pre-resurrection announcement of the Messiah's authority
(28:19).

Judas was quite likely an adherent of the Zealot sect known as sicarii,
i.e., dagger-bearers. The group comprised intensely fanatical national-
ists bent on political revolution. Barabbus may have been a member of
the sect as well (27:15f). Thirty shekels was the price of a slave (Exodus 21:32). Judas bides his time as the Son of Man awaits his time.

Passover was eaten after sunset (Exodus 12). The meal itself poignantly
symbolized divine deliverance of Israel from suffering, serfdom and
slavery. While the bald betrayal by Judas fulfills Scripture, it in no way
relieves him of responsibility for his deliberate treachery (26:14–16).

Feast of the New Covenant 26:26–29

Jesus presides over Passover as head of the household. As he takes bread
he speaks the ancient Hebrew prayer of thanksgiving: Blessed are you,
Lord God, King of the universe, who brings forth from the earth. Preceding this prayer, Psalms 113–114 were intoned as part of the ritual,
along with an explanation of the significance of the elements used in
the meal. Jesus adds words, which are totally and strikingly new. Of the
unleavened bread he says, "This is my body." Jesus speaks another blessing: (Greek: eucharistia, thanksgiving) over the cup: Blessed are you,
Lord God, King of the universe, creator of the fruit of the vine. Three,
often four cups of wine were drunk at the meal. The wine Jesus gives
his disciples to share is identified as his blood of the new covenant,
poured out for the remission of sins. Blood was an essential element of
the old covenant (Exodus 24:8). It played a prominent part in the sac-

rificial cults of Israel (Leviticus 16). Announcement of a new covenant at once reminds the disciples of the words of Jeremiah 31:31–34. They constitute people of the new age, which will attain glorious fulfillment in the banquet of salvation (8:11).

God's delivering Servant has celebrated the final Passover. His community celebrates the feast of forgiveness pledged by the new covenant. It is participation in the Messiah's death, a thanksgiving (Eucharist) of the redeemed community, which praises God for deliverance from the bondage of sin through the life, death and resurrection of Jesus as it waits for the return of the glorified and exalted Lord. The Church lives in God's forgiveness; it awaits his final vindication (25:34).

Way of the Cross 26:30–27:56

Psalms 113–118 form the Hebrew Hallel. Jesus and his disciples sing this Passover hymn on the way to the Mount of Olives. Jesus cites Zechariah 13:7. His impending sufferings and condemnation will so greatly offend his disciples that they will forsake and deny him. In obtuse contradiction of Jesus' words, Peter demurs. The others share his confident bravado that he will never fall away. Cocks normally crowed between the hours of midnight and 3:00 a.m. That watch of the night was appropriately named, cockcrow.

Gethsemane 26:36–56

The familiar garden known as Gethsemane (lit: olive vat, press) lay on the far side of the Kidron Valley. Peter, James and John witness the deep anguish of Jesus' physical and spiritual struggles. Jesus alludes to Psalms 42:6 and 53:5. As the magnitude of the Passion oppresses him, he cries out to his Father in heaven (6:9). He seeks relief and release. Yet he is prepared to drink deeply the cup of suffering (20:22f). Jesus had taught his disciples to pray, Lead us not into testing. At this crucial hour of the Messiah's ministry, they are being tested. Their spirit may be strong; their physical strength does not match it. Realizing that the inevitable hour of deliverance has come and strengthened by his own prayer, Jesus confidently consigns himself to the Father's gracious will. Matthew wants to make it unmistakably clear that Jesus is in control of the situation. Even as he is seized by the motley mob, he asserts his authority. The prophetic Scriptures must be fulfilled. Jesus bluntly warns all zealous, but misguided followers, that in taking the sword to defend his ministry they may, in reality, be acting contrary to the express will of God.

The Sanhedrin 26:57–27:1

The way to the cross first leads to Caiaphas, High Priest of Israel. The supreme court of Israel was composed of seventy-one Scribes, Sadducees, Pharisees and elders. It was responsible for Jewish religious matters, a right granted by Rome. A formal assembly (veiled reference to Psalm 2:2) in order to judge a capital offense was illegal. Soliciting of false witnesses against Jesus may therefore have taken the form of a preliminary hearing. The formal trial was most likely held the following morning (27:1–2). Guards were Temple police assigned to the High Priest who presided over the court.

Two witnesses were the minimum required by Jewish law. Any threat to destroy the Temple would be construed as blasphemy since the Temple represented Yahweh's name and presence with his people (Exodus 20:7). Penalty for blasphemy was death. Jesus assumes the role of the suffering Servant portrayed in Isaiah 53:7. Speaking under solemn oath, Jesus identifies himself by means of a clear allusion to Psalm 110:1–2. Caiaphas accuses him of the capital crime of blasphemy. He fully realizes the claim, which Jesus has made. The formal charges brought against Jesus are both political and religious in nature. The Council passed judgment because Jesus affirmed, under oath, that he is the Messiah. Their accusation before the Roman governor labeled Jesus a political revolutionary who would cause the people to rise up in revolt against Rome. This constituted the capital crime of seditious treason.

Jewish law required that sessions of the Sanhedrin involving the death penalty be separated by a sunset, i.e., a full day. Such trials could not be undertaken the day before the Sabbath or special festival since this requirement could not be met. This supports the supposition that the assembly, which was hastily convened the night before was a preliminary arraignment.

Pontius Pilate 27:2–31

The man whose name became part of the great creeds of the Church served as procurator of Judea A.D. 26–36. God's Servant is now in the hands of Gentiles (20:19; 26:2). Condemned by the Roman court on the charge of sedition (27:11; 27–29; 37), he is sentenced to death by crucifixion. Before Matthew recounts details of the trial, he inserts into his narrative the return of the blood money by disillusioned Judas. The decision of the Sanhedrin is decisive. It has found Jesus guilty of blasphemy. Matthew sees in the incident references to Jeremiah 32:6–15 and Zechariah 11:12f. Judas reaps the bitter fruit of his betrayal (26:15, 24).

The trial was likely held at the old fortress palace of Herod, located west of the city. Herod ruled by imperial favor. Pilate faces the sticky matter of exercising royal rule in Judea apart from imperial appointment. Impressed by Jesus' demeanor and response to the specific charge brought against him, Pilate resorts to a practice he had obviously followed in the past. The custom of paschal amnesty apparently originated during the Hasmonean period. The Mishnah refers to it. Roman authorities permitted the practice whenever it was to their advantage to do so. The governor allows the crowd to make the choice.

Barabbas (Aramaic: bar, son; abbas, of a father) was a condemned murderer. He undoubtedly belonged to the fanatic Zealots. Some ancient manuscripts of this Gospel refer to him as Jesus Barabbas. If so, the choice of the multitudes is laden with truly poignant significance. Jesus, criminal son of his father, is set free. Jesus, Messiah-Son of the heavenly Father, is condemned to die. Symbolic washing of hands was basically a Hebrew custom (Deuteronomy 21:6). Pilate cunningly seeks to avoid risky political involvement. Though Matthew does not record them, the presiding magistrate often spoke the words, "away to the cross."

The witness of the New Testament and the early Church is that the trial of Jesus before Pilate followed usual legal form. The trial is public, charges are formally brought and the accused is reminded of the right self-defense. Roman law even stipulated that the accused have at least three opportunities to speak to the charge. Judges were permitted to seek counsel from others. Sentences were formally pronounced from the official tribunal (bema). Jesus stands condemned. The Council condemned him for claiming to be the Messiah without God's validation. Pilate condemned him for claiming to be king without Caesar's validation.

Golgotha 27:32–54

Golgotha (Aramaic: hill of execution; Greek: *kraniou*, place of skull; Latin: Calvary) was a mound located beyond the city walls. Matthew's account of the Messiah's crucifixion is couched in rich Old Testament imagery. The Sanhedrin mocks Jesus, invoking words of Psalm 22:8 in an attempt to justify its shameful behavior (27:41–43). Jesus is offered wine mixed with gall and given a sponge full of vinegar (Psalm 69:21). Lots are cast for his clothing (Psalm 22:18). He hangs between two criminals (Isaiah 53:12). He endures jeers of the passing crowds and taunting insults from those crucified with him (Psalms 22:7–18; 69:9). Significant phenomena accompany the Messiah's death. Eerie darkness covers the land from 12:00 P.M. to 3:00 P.M. The veil separating the Holy Place from the Holy of Holies in the Temple is ripped from top to bottom (Exodus 26:31–35). An earthquake shatters rock and opens tombs, messianic signs of the end of the age (Isaiah 24:19–20; 26:19; Daniel 12:2–3). The crowd assembled at the foot of the cross mistakenly believes that Jesus is calling for Elijah (2 Kings 2:9–12).

Matthew's record is faithful to the theme he has so heavily and constantly emphasized. Jesus is the Messiah, Son of the living God (16:16). Commentators identify seven words from the cross. Matthew includes in his account that generally known as the fourth word. In agonizing depths of humiliation, he utters a prayer of trust for vindication (Psalm 22:1). He does not address the Father in heaven with intimate, abba, but with Eli (Hebrew: Eliya, my God). At the beginning of his ministry, divine Sonship with the Father is attested (3:17). At its close, it is attested once again (27:54).

Crucifixion was an excessively cruel method of execution. It was practiced not only by the imperial government of Rome, but was known among ancient Persians, Greeks and Jews as well. In Jesus' day it was recognized as one of the basest and most inhumane forms of death, reserved for the worst and lowliest of criminals.

The Tomb 27:55–66

Among those witnessing the Messiah's death are the faithful women. Matthew names Mary of Magdala, Mary the mother of James and Joseph and the mother of James and John. Roman custom dictated that a corpse remain on the cross until decay set in. Hebrew law dictated that the body be removed before nightfall (Deuteronomy 21:22f). Joseph, hailing from the village of Arimathea, receives permission for immediate burial. Jewish corpses were always anointed prior to burial. Tombs, hewn out of rock, were located outside the city. While sealing a tomb with a heavy stone was normal practice, the seal placed at Joseph's tomb is perhaps an allusion to Daniel 6:16f. The guard is stationed at the sepulcher in response to a specific request. Matthew's witness is unmistakably clear. No one was able to steal the body from the cross. No one was able to remove it from the tomb.

Discussion

1. Contrast Passover and Eucharist. Which features are similar? What is totally new and different?

2. Contrast the actions of an unnamed woman and a named disciple. How does each serve as a powerful symbol and example?

3. Contrast the actions of the Sanhedrin and Pilate. For what claims was Jesus sentenced to die?

4. What firm assurance does Matthew provide that Jesus actually died upon his cross and that his body was not stolen from the tomb?

CHAPTER FIFTEEN

Resurrection of the Messiah
Matthew 28:1–20

Belief in the resurrection of Jesus from the dead was an integral component of Christian proclamation and witness long before the narrative was recorded and the Gospels were composed. The book known as the Acts of the Apostles relates how Jesus presented himself alive after the Passion by infallible proofs. He was seen by the apostles for forty days after his rising from the grave and testified of the kingdom of God (1:3). The conviction that Jesus, true to his promises, was raised up the third day was boldly and decisively witnessed by the messianic community in preaching, teaching, hymns, spiritual songs, worship, creedal statements, celebration of the eucharist and oral tradition. This deep conviction was faithfully transmitted. St. Paul defines the good news of God acting in the life, death and resurrection of his Messiah to reconcile the world to himself (2 Corinthians 5:18–21) as the message he had received (1 Corinthians 15:1–4).

The earliest testimony to proclamation of the resurrection of Christ is probably the message delivered on the day of Pentecost. Jesus was delivered up to be crucified. God raised him because death was unable to hold him. Peter marshaled evidence from the Old Testament confirming the reality of the resurrection. Filled, as were all within the community, with the Holy Spirit Peter maintains that David foresaw and spoke of the resurrection of the Messiah in Psalms 16:8–11 and 89:3,4,35,36 (Acts 2:25–31).

Christ is Risen! 28:1–15
Matthew, in concert with other Gospels, does not provide a lengthy or detailed description of the resurrection event. He affirms the message heard by women who early Sunday morning went to the tomb. The angel of the Lord had rolled back the stone, which sealed the sepulcher. Matching the appearance of the transfigured Messiah (17:2), the angel proclaimed the staggering truth of Easter victory. Jesus is not

here! He is risen as he said! The accompanying earthquake serves not only as a messianic sign to believers (27:51–54; Daniel 6:23); it provides evidence for the guards who relate to the chief priests all that has occurred. These priests and elders, who had so easily resorted to slander and treachery, find it so easy to resort to bribery. Their fraudulent course of action establishes the rumor that the disciples had somehow stolen the corpse. That bit of deceit, intended to counter the claim that Jesus had risen, was repeated as true by enemies of the Church and the gospel well into the second century and even beyond.

No single segment of the Gospels has evoked greater interest, criticism, controversy and thorough investigation than its decisive witness to the resurrection of Jesus Christ. Neither the Gospels nor other writings of the New Testament describe the emergence of Jesus from the tomb. Neither do they assert that the disciples or anyone else came to believe in the resurrection because they found the tomb empty. The disciples are indeed told the good news by women who immediately share and eagerly share it (28:9–10). They are convinced of the resurrection as the living Christ appears to them. Just so the messianic community of every age is convinced of it as the living Christ is revealed in the word, which proclaims: He is risen, as he said (28:6).

The resurrection of Jesus the Messiah continues to be the foundation of the Christian faith and the heart of the good news (gospel) of redemption, deliverance and salvation. In bold witness to the reality of the resurrection, St. Paul declares and writes that Christ died for our sins according to the Scriptures, that he was buried and that he was raise on the third day according to the Scriptures. He argues cogently and convincingly that if the Messiah has not been raised, Christian proclamation is a sham and Christian faith is totally useless. In fact, if Christ has not been raised, we are still in our sins. Those who died trusting in Christ have actually perished. Thank God Christ has been raised (1 Corinthians 15:3–20).

Enthronement of the Messiah 28:16–20
As he had promised (26:32), Jesus appears to his disciples in Galilee (28:16ff). He had conducted an essential part of his ministry in Galilee (4:12–23; cf. 28:7,10). The commission he entrusts to the apostles and his church is to be a continuation of that prophetic ministry. Jesus has

already assured the community of his presence with them (18:20). He reassures them of that presence to the very close of the age (28:20).

The mandate to go forth and make of all the nations disciples, pupils and followers of the Risen One is frequently entitled the Great Commission. It is to be carried out by baptizing and teaching. Baptism (Greek: Bapitzein, wash, cleanse) is the sacrament of initiation into the messianic community. It commits one to growth in discipleship. Ceremonial washings, ablutions and ritual purifications were practiced not only by Jews (Exodus 30:17; 1 Kings 7:38) in their own worship practices and reception of proselytes; they were used by pagan cults and various mystery religions as initiatory rites. Christian baptism is the application of water in the name of the Father, Son and Holy Spirit. Though there is abundant evidence that early Christian baptism was administered in the name of the Lord Jesus (Acts 2:38), the Trinitarian force was well established by the end of the first century.

The Messiah's commission to baptize and teach is the program conferred on the community by virtue of his sweeping authority. In the resurrection, he received from his Father in heaven that universal and eternal dominion foretold in Daniel 7:13f. Jesus bestows upon his community power to act in his name. He promises his presence to uphold and sustain as his people faithfully carry his program out.

Discussion

1. Who first announced the resurrection of our Lord?

2. Does faith in the resurrection of Christ from the dead arise from proof of an empty tomb or from the word of proclamation: He is risen?

3. How did applying water in the name of the Triune God come to be called Baptism?

4. What is the lasting significance of the messianic ministry of Jesus? What above all else declares that the ministry of Jesus was truly valid and that we are not to look for another?

Conclusion

The Gospel of Matthew has achieved its purpose. It concludes with themes, which are basic to the Christian faith as confessed by the early community of believers surrounding the resurrected Messiah. Its prologue declares that Jesus the Messiah is the son of David, the son of Abraham (1:1), key figures in the covenant history of Israel. As the narrative continues, Matthew recounts the discourse, which reveals that Israel's Messiah is the ultimate son of David because he is, at the same time, David's Lord (22:41–45; cf. 2 Samuel 7:14–16). Jesus is the child of Yahweh's promises (1:20–21; cf. Genesis 18:1–15). He is, in fact, Emmanuel: God is with us (1:23; cf. Isaiah 7:14), come to be Savior of all. Early on, Gentiles from the east acknowledge and worship him (2:2). After the resurrection, women and disciples do likewise (28:9,17). At his baptism, the Messiah is declared to be God's beloved Son (3:17; cf. 16:16; 17:5). In his enthronement, he is declared to possess all authority in heaven and on earth (28:18). At the onset of his ministry, people were amazed at his teaching for it bore the unmistakable marks of authority (7:28). At the close of his ministry, he exercises his authority to continue his teaching (28:20).

The dynamic thrust of Matthew's record is that God has decisively intervened in our history, in our world, in our age. He has done so in the messianic ministry of Jesus.

Resources

Selected readings from Luther's Large Catechism of 1529 and other Lutheran confessions are suggested as reflections upon the biblical record. Citations are by page and paragraph of the edition included in Theodore G. Tappert's translation of the *Book of Concord* of 1580 (Muhlenberg Press, 1959).

Chapter 1: Beginnings of the Gospel of Jesus the Messiah

1. Jesus became man, conceived and born without sin of the Holy Spirit and the Virgin (414,31).
2. I believe that Jesus Christ, true Son of God, has become my Lord (414,27).

Chapter 2: Beginnings of the Ministry of the Messiah

1. Jesus has redeemed me from sin (414,27).
2. Before this I had no Lord and King (414,27).

Chapter 3: The Law and the Prophets

1. Lack of fear of God and trust in him transgress the first table of the Decalog (102,14).
2. It is foolish to imagine that we are justified by the works of the second table (138,224).

Chapter 4: Living as People of God

1. We cannot correctly keep the law of God unless by faith we have the Spirit (125,1342).
2. God is pleased when we keep the law (126,140).

Chapter 5: Authority of the Messiah

1. The true voice of the gospel is absolution (187,39).
2. What is the office of the keys? (311,1).

Chapter 6: Apostleship and Discipleship

1. Christ gave the apostles only spiritual power (325,31).

2. Acknowledging Christ is being acknowledged by Christ (614,17).

Chapter 7: Jesus, Revelation of the Father

1. God has completely given himself to us in Christ (413,26).

2. Christ is God and man in once indivisible person (489,18).

Chapter 8: The Kingdom of God

1. Christ's kingdom is spiritual, not political (222,2).

2. What is the kingdom of God? (426,51).

Chapter 9: Son of the Living God

1. Worshipping Jesus in vain (493,3).

2. The church is built upon the confession made by Peter (342,25).

Chapter 10: Life in the Kingdom

1. Christ has commanded us to absolve one another from sin (458,14).

2. Good works must necessarily be done by God's people (133,189; 552,7).

Chapter 11: David's Son is David's Lord

1. Christ is the reigning king of heaven (499,20).

2. The Commandments are the fountain from which all good work springs (407,311).

Chapter 12: Apostasy of Israel

1. We do not have the Commandments merely for display purposes (410,331).

2. One who despises the word of God finds no comfort in the grace of God (532,57).

Chapter 13: End of the Age

1. Do our good works preserve faith and salvation? (555,30).

2. Christ praises faithful business people (229,4).

Chapter 14: Passion of the Messiah

1. Christ has made us free and restored us to the Father's favor and grace (414,30).

2. Christ swallowed up and devoured death (414,31).

Chapter 15: Resurrection of the Messiah

1. He rose from the dead and assumed dominion at the right hand of the Father (414,31).

2. The entire gospel depends upon proper understanding of the birth, passion, resurrection and ascension of Christ. Salvation is based upon it (415,32).

The Christian Faith

According to the Gospel of Mark

Introduction

The Gospel According to Mark confronts us as decisive testimony to the faith of the early Christian community. Led by the Spirit of God, this community confessed that in the life, death and resurrection of Jesus the Messiah, God reveals his saving action for humankind. While not the earliest record of the ministry of Jesus, Mark is an early written witness to that ministry. Indeed, it is commonly held that Mark is the earliest of the four Gospels, which found place in the canon of the New Testament. Most scholars opt for a date of A.D. 65–70 as reliably certain for its composition.

Certain characteristics of this Gospel fit remarkably well into a design to view it as a manual of instruction. The notion that one of the Gospels can serve as an instructional tool is neither new nor novel. Mark was composed to provide material for the preaching ministry of the early church. It is renowned for its vivid, fast-moving and straightforward narrative style. Yet it was never intended to serve as a biographical or strictly chronological account of Jesus' life or ministry. It testifies to the good news of salvation. As it does so, it summons its readers of every age to confess Jesus as their own Messiah and Lord.

Near the close of the first Christian century, Clement of Rome, writing to the church in Corinth, refers to the apostles as evangelists sent out by Christ. The sacred writings are literary products of that missionary movement. Near the close of the second century, Clement of Alexandria suggests that Mark produced the Gospel, which bears his name in direct response to urging by the church. He was to record all that he recalled of the preaching of Peter. An earlier contemporary, Irenaeus, describes Mark as the interpreter of Peter. For the late second century, Papias of Hieropolis testifies that Mark wrote down accurately, but not strict, literary or systematic order, all that he remembered of what Christ had said and done. This he learned from Peter who molded his message to the needs of his hearers, not with an eye to drawing up in connected form sayings of the Lord.

A winning characteristic of Mark is its clear portrait of Jesus the Messiah. Mark introduces us to a truly human Jesus. He experiences weariness, anger, distress, suffering, sorrow, but also deep feelings of compassion and mercy. At the same time, Jesus is the Son of God who came to offer his life as a ransom for the sinful humankind. An alternative ending to the Gospel inserts these words of the risen Lord: I was delivered into death on behalf of sinners...that they might inherit the glory of righteousness in heaven (16:14–15). A related characteristic is Mark's forceful witness to the cross and resurrection. This Gospel may lack systematic order. But it demonstrates a powerful dramatic pattern. While it details nothing of Jesus' birth, background, boyhood or early life in Nazareth, Mark does know something of the Messiah's family. But this Gospel is an eminently theological document. It boldly proclaims Jesus as Messiah (Christ), Savior and Lord. That clear affirmation is proclaimed in the sufferings, forsakenness, crucifixion and resurrection of the one who began his ministry by proclaiming that the kingdom has come (1:15).

A careful examination reveals that Mark is a notably competent writer. He carefully plots the structure of his record. He depicts the ministry of Jesus in terms of preparation, popularity, conflict, abandonment, tragedy and triumph. Each scene of the drama leads in its own way to the climax sounded that first Good Friday by the centurion who exclaims: Truly this man was the Son of God! (15:39).

Material presented in this study is largely non-technical in nature. Problems dealing with authorship, sources, forms, process and relationship with other Gospels are best left to scholars and their continuing research. Non-Markan references are intentionally kept to a minimum. Most reliable translations include cross-references to parallel readings in the Synoptics (Matthew and Luke) and in John. The reader may find them useful. One problem does call for at least a brief comment. Jesus is early identified as the Messiah. There appears to be no secret attached to this forthright claim. Yet Jesus enjoins silence with regard to compelling messianic claims. This is the so-called messianic secret. His understanding of his role differs markedly from popularly held notions spawned by centuries of social, political and religious factors. The secrecy motif prevented a premature and politically disastrous movement, which would have deterred Jesus from his true mission.

Little more needs to be said regarding authorship. Tradition came to associate each Gospel with a specific writer. It is fairly uniform in attributing this work to Mark, son of Mary, nephew of Barnabas, sometime associate of Paul and confidant of Peter (Acts 12:12, 25; 13:13; Colossians 4:10; 2 Timothy 4:11; 1 Peter 5:13). Tradition further cites Rome as place of origin. The appearance of Latinisms, use of Roman time, explanation of Hebrew customs and consistent translation of Aramaic expressions all point to a predominantly Gentile audience. Perhaps the Christian community in Rome commissioned Mark to write during the very time Nero was launching his bestial persecutions, A.D. 64–68. Some three hundred years later, Jerome maintains that Mark was asked by fellow Christians in Rome to write a short Gospel, which might be read in all the churches.

This is the Gospel According to Mark. It is a book of unknown title, date and authorship. But the whole church confesses it to be an apostolic and authoritative witness to Jesus, God's Messiah and our Savior. For this reason it is a continuing witness to the good news that in Christ the kingdom of God has indeed come. Repent and believe the good news! (1:14–15).

For use within Lutheran congregations or by other interested persons or groups, selected readings from Martin Luther's Large Catechism of 1529 are listed for each chapter in the Resources. Citations are by page and paragraph of Theodore G. Tappert's translation of the *Book of Concord* (Muhenberg Press, 1959). They are intended to encourage exploration of Luther's powerful witness to what he identifies as the heritage of Christendom from ancient times.

Part One

Power and Popularity

CHAPTER ONE

The Good News
Mark 1:1–34

Jesus is the Messiah 1:1–13

Mark is a witness to the gospel, the message and proclamation that Jesus is the Messiah, the Son of God (9:2–8). That is good news. In him, God has fulfilled his promises. Messiah is not, strictly speaking, a name, but a title (Hebrew: Anointed; Greek: Christ). To confess Jesus Christ is to believe that Jesus of Nazareth is the promised Messiah. Mark employs language of the Old Testament to introduce the messianic messenger. He cites Exodus 23:20, Isaiah 40:3 and Malachi 3:1. John preaches repentance for the remission of sins. Repentance and confession are directed to God. Forgiveness is God's response to the confession of sin and guilt. Baptism is literally an application of water. It cleanses and purifies. Gentiles who adopted Judaism received a baptism of initiation to symbolize cleansing from a former non-Jewish way of life.

John summoned his hearers to baptism as preparation for the messianic kingdom. After his resurrection, Jesus authorized his disciples to proclaim the gospel to all, promising that whoever believes and is baptized shall be saved (16:14–16). The church proclaims forgiveness to all who acknowledge and confess their sins and see in the life, death and resurrection of Jesus, God's gracious act of deliverance and pardon. Through this ministry, the Messiah "baptizes" with the Holy Spirit who calls people to confess Jesus as Lord and Savior.

Jesus receives baptism from John, though he required neither personal repentance nor forgiveness. The New Testament clearly portrays Jesus as the sinless Son of God. His baptism rather denotes his complete identification with sinful humankind. It also signals the beginning of his messianic ministry. In former times, God spoke through prophets. Now he speaks through his Son. The manifestation of the Holy Spirit strengthens Jesus' conviction that he indeed is the Messiah. Note the witness to the Trinitarian confession of the church. The Father speaks, the Son is baptized, the Holy Spirit comes upon him.

This divine witness is immediately challenged. In narrating this incident, Mark uses the Greek word euthus (immediately). He employs this term forty-one times, ten times in the first chapter of the Gospel. A number of commentators suggest that Mark is breathlessly running through the story of the Messiah's ministry in order to capture its vividness, spontaneity and dynamism. The Messiah's ministry must be proclaimed!

The Spirit literally casts Jesus out in the desert wilderness. There, in that bleak, inhospitable, arid region Jesus is tested. Satan is the dread adversary. His opposition to divine rule is revealed in disease, suffering, seduction, temptation to sin, doubt of God's promises, misbelief and unbelief. Reference to beasts may hint of the messianic age when all creation, it was believed, would be restored to pristine harmony and peace (Isaiah 1:6–9). Angers minister to Jesus during that stressful period. God's people are assured that God never forsakes his own!

Ministering the Gospel 1:14–22

The gospel is the good news. It is the joyous message of forgiveness, peace, hope, truth and life in Christ. The Messiah preaches repentance, a change of mind and heart. He proclaims faith, which is trust in God's word of pardon. The church is commissioned by Christ to do the same (16:15–16). Whenever the gospel is proclaimed and shared, the kingdom of God comes.

Jesus calls his first disciples with a simple but imperious word: Follow me! A disciple obediently follows. A disciple also learns from the teacher. Those called by Jesus learned that following him entails serving. Jesus served that those who follow might learn to serve him (10:45). The Temple in Jerusalem was the spiritual center of Judaism. It was designated a house of prayer (11:17). Synagogues were local houses of prayer and teaching (12:38–39). On a particular Sabbath, Jesus acts as rabbi of the day. This indicates that the community recognized in him a qualified teacher of Torah, divine law embodied in the Pentateuch and summarized in the holy ten words from Sinai. Jesus teaches with such moral vigor and persuasiveness that the congregation is completely astonished. Here is a fresh, authoritative voice! He does not merely mouth rabbinic tradition. He is a teacher sent by God.

Initial Messianic Victories 1:23–34

His authority is buttressed by his healing of a demoniac. The unclean spirit confesses that Jesus of Nazareth is the Holy One of God and obeys his word. Unclean spirits were deemed to be demons who could inflict terrible spiritual and physical harm. Exorcisms were attempted by means of secret formulae, incantations and bizarre religious rites. One of the signs of the messianic age was victory over demonism.

The Messiah heals the mother-in-law of Peter by means of another powerful word. Jesus clearly separates himself from so-called faith healers, both old and contemporary, who require vast audiences in order to perform. He demonstrates as well that he does not dabble in pseudo-religious or pseudo-medical practices, which often confuse and even destroy the faith of those who seek them out.

At the conclusion of the Sabbath, vast crowds gather around him. Jesus is compassionate. He responds to human misery and need. But it must be asked whether the Messiah's ministry is already being misunderstood. He forbids the demons to speak. For the moment, at least, he wants to dissuade people from seeing in him a miracle-worker to be used, rather than a Messiah to be followed. Our Lord never wants to be viewed merely as a kind spiritual superman who is ready to solve all of life's problems for the asking.

Discussion:

1. How does Mark concisely define the gospel?

2. How does the church today minister in the name of Christ?

CHAPTER TWO

The Messiah in Ministry
Mark 1:35–3:35

Ministry in Galilee 1:35–2:12

Galilee was a province of the Roman Empire, ruled by Herod Antipas, a son of Herod the Great who had reigned over most of Palestine. Both held office as the pleasure of the Roman emperor. A procurator governed Judea. Since the people had no real king of their own, messianic hopes turned from spiritual to purely political aspirations. Dreams of a messianic golden age surrendered to revolutionary plots to reclaim the ancient throne of David. The Galilean mission must have lasted several months. Mark closely links prayer with healing and preaching. Jesus shares our humanity. As a true human being he was dependent on his heavenly Father and was in need of continuous fellowship with him. This is especially apparent in Gethsemane when Jesus seeks strength to carry out his Father's will (14:32–42).

The Messiah came to redeem and bring healing to the whole person. Leprosy was a loathsome and highly contagious skin malady. It led to banishment from family and friends. Contrary to both law and custom, Jesus affects healing, but directs the cleansed leper to fulfill Mosaic requirements (Leviticus 14). Jesus notes the faith of those who bore a paralytic to him. He speaks the gospel in capsule form: Your sins are forgiven. Psychosomatic medicine is not a modern phenomenon. Elements of Jewish theology perceived an integral connection between sin, guilt, suffering and sickness. Since sin causes sickness, there can be no healing apart from divine forgiveness. Only God is able to impart this. For Jesus to make such a claim was not only totally outrageous; it was blasphemous! Sin is indeed spiritual disease. But not every illness is to be attributed to specific sins. As the Messiah, Jesus is healer of body and spirit. His forgiveness mediates peace with God. He meets his adversaries on their own ground. This man is sick. I forgive him. He is cured. The Messiah's claim is justified!

Another Disciple is Chosen 2:13–22

Jesus launches a three-pronged ministry of preaching, healing and teaching. Jewish rabbis often taught as they walked. A lakeshore served as an ideal classroom, as did village streets, homes, open-air places, boats and synagogues. Levi was in the employ of Herod Antipas. Levi, named by Mark as the son of Alphaeus, and possibly a brother of the "other" James (3:18), is elsewhere identified as Matthew (10:3). Tax collectors were uniformly despised by the people. Not only did they serve repressive regimes; they extorted additional revenue from the masses. That Jesus would befriend Levi and call him to become a collector of people for the messianic kingdom was beyond imagination. The Messiah breaks one taboo after another. First, he chooses Levi to be a disciple. Then he shares a fellowship meal with Levi and his circle of companions labeled by religious the religious community as sinners. In Hebrew thought, they did not live according to the laws and traditions of the elders. When Jesus is condemned by Pharisees, his answer is remarkably pointed. Physicians minister to those who are ill. Those who think they are righteous and whole in the sight of God feel no need for one who had come to seek and save the lost. Early in the Messiah's ministry, we detect strong undercurrents of opposition.

Mark's reference to fasting was perhaps occasioned by the feast prepared at Levi's house. As a spiritual exercise, fasting was prescribed only for the great Day of Atonement. Stricter Jews were fond of observing more days. In Jesus' time, Mondays and Thursdays were normally set aside. Unfortunately, the practice soon became means for acquiring merit before God and approval in the sight of people. Reference to the marriage celebration contains a profound nuance. Jesus is the heavenly bridegroom in whose ministry God's kingdom has arrived. His gospel of grace, forgiveness, joy and peace bursts the pretensions of all who are smugly satisfied with a religion rooted in legalism and tradition.

Lord of the Sabbath 2:23–3:6

To the pious in Israel, few things were more demanding of careful observance than the Sabbath. Rules and regulations had multiplied in attempting to build a protective hedge about its sanctity. To pick heads of grain as one walked through the fields was allowed (Deuteronomy 23:25). But according to rabbinical tradition, reaping, winnowing and threshing were not permitted on the Sabbath. In response, Jesus cites the familiar story narrated in 1 Samuel 21:1–6. Rules often get in the way of spiritual worship. Religious practices, which are forced upon worshippers, can divert them from loving, willing response to the grace of God. Furthermore, humankind is more important than Sabbath regulations. He who came to fulfill the law of God is Lord of the Sabbath. In order to strengthen that bold assertion, Jesus then does what Pharisees deemed utterly unthinkable. On the Sabbath, in the very synagogue where the law and traditions were extolled and honored, Jesus restores to a man (very likely a stonemason) the ability to earn his living. Isn't that in accord with the true sense of Sabbath celebration? Blind, fanatical and misguided religious zeal often leads to strange extremes. In this instance, Pharisees were intent upon up-holding! The Messiah may be approaching the zenith of power and popularity. Opposition from some grows stronger.

Ministering to Multitudes 3:7–35

Hordes from Jewish and non-Jewish communities now seek him out. The sick and possessed literally press upon him. As his popularity mushrooms, Jesus utters a cautionary note. Messiahship involves more than physical healing. Likewise discipleship involves more than being healed. A premature announcement or an overly zealous enthusiasm may trigger rebellion against Rome. Such could spell disaster for the messianic movement and tighten bonds of political suppression. Some forty years later, a revolt fueled by a fanatical freedom movement re-sulted in the total destruction of Jerusalem by the armies of Rome.

Jesus turns from the many to the few. He calls twelve to carry his mes-sage and mission to the multitudes. They are disciples who must fol-low and learn. They are apostles, literally sent-out ones, who will rep-resent his cause. And they are a diverse group. At least one, Simon is a Cananaean, member of the Zealot sect, which pledged to rid Palestine of its foreign masters by means of murder and revolution. As Jesus at-tracts these disciples, he at the same time, attracts those who, at the time, will not follow. Friends and even family accuse him of taking leave of his senses. Scribes representing the Sanhedrin in Jerusalem, men trained in Jewish and experienced experts in their traditions, ac-tually take leave of their senses. In spiritual blindness, they accuse Jesus of casting out lesser demons in the power and authority of the major demon. Persistent enmity against Christ results in strange actions and illogical conclusions. In reality, they are resisting the Holy Spirit. In hardhearted opposition, they adamantly refuse to acknowledge the truth even as the Spirit of God convincingly reveals it. All sins, even those of unbelief and opposition, can be forgiven as one repents and clings to the promise of grace offered to all in the gospel. Blaspheming the Holy Spirit makes that impossible.

In marked contrast, those led by the Spirit who anointed the Messiah at his baptism (1:9–11), joyfully and confidently confess him as Savior and Lord. They are the Messiah's true family. Our Lord does not demean, neither does he disown, his own natural family, even though they come close to demeaning and disowning him. He simply makes it clear that in the kingdom of his Father, spiritual ties of faith and obedience are more important. They are precious and more blessed than physical ones.

Discussion:

1. Compare a legalistic (what must I do to gain favor with God) with an evangelical (what has God done for me) approach to faith and life.

2. Is there a basic difference between a disciple and an apostle? In what sense do these terms apply to all Christians? In what sense do they not apply?

3. Is it possible to seek wrong things from Jesus? From one's profession of him as Lord?

CHAPTER THREE

The Messiah Teaches in Parables
Mark 4: 1–41

Sowing the Seed of the Word 4:1–34

Mark introduces a new methodology employed as eager crowds continue to press on Jesus. The Messiah resorts to the age-old parabolic technique so capably used by Old Testament writer and various rabbinical schools. Parables are comparison narratives. The effectively drive home specific lessons regarding the kingdom of God inaugurated by Messiah's ministry (1:14–15). Parables serve to compel the hearer to discover and apply lessons being inculcated. That is why parables must be interpreted within their own context. Hearers must ask: What is the trust of this particular parable? What is its central point of comparison? What is it proclaiming about the kingdom of God? What is it saying to me? For Jesus begins this aspect of his teaching with an emphatic word: Listen! (4:3, 9, 23, 24).

The parable of the sower provides the Messiah's own understanding of the nature and purpose of the parabolic method. He speaks of the secret or mystery of the kingdom. Major Greek and Roman cities boasted cults and societies known as mystery religions. They generally offered insight into hidden secrets or mysteries of the universe. Some even promised immortality. Adherents initiated into the cult experienced a new birth, which symbolized movement from spiritual ignorance to truth. They were supposedly put in touch with the god or gods to which the cult was dedicated. One such mystery religion, the cult of the goddess Isis, promised freedom from the blind fate, which ruled human destiny. Rites and rituals were often connected with the use of hallucinatory drugs. Those who remained outside the cult remained in spiritual darkness.

Mysteries of the kingdom of God are understood by all who have spiritual eyes and ears to comprehend the message the Messiah is bringing. The citation from Isaiah 6:9–10 reminds even them, however, that cir-

cumstances may block right understanding of that message. Many im-
pediments seek to choke the very life of the word. Yet it must be sown.
The Messiah himself offers assurance that the seeds will bear fruit.

Within this context, Mark relates four very vivid and pithy logia of
Jesus. Each extends our understanding of his mission and ministry. A
lamp brings light. Jesus is the light of the world. He alone can dispel
spiritual darkness and ignorance. Those who follow him as disciples reflect his light in their faith and life. God reveals the good news of grace
and forgiveness in Christ. We are to hear the gospel when it is proclaimed. The good news is to be received with obedient faith. Those
who respond are to lead lives pleasing to God and will reap a harvest
of blessings.

Those called into the kingdom must also grow in knowledge of the
world. Neglect of such growth leads to ultimate loss of what they had.
Jesus unfolds the meaning of his parables and sayings with compassion
and patience. Disciples are really learners. All who remain with him –
after the merely curious have left – reap the blessings of his teachings.

Lord of Nature 4:35–41

Disciples of the Messiah have witnessed his dynamic authority in the
expulsion of demons, healing of all manner of sickness and forgiving of
sins. Now he exhibits power that overwhelms and even terrifies them.
Lake Galilee, known also as Gennesaret, was susceptible to sudden and
violent storms. As one such explosive storm overtakes the disciples,
they fear for their lives, even though they are experienced and seasoned fishermen. Jesus rebukes their fractured faith. At the same time,
he commands the turbulent wind and sea to give way to a great calm.
He employs the same word he addressed to the demoniac in the synagogue of Capernaum (1:25).

Jesus is Lord of the elements. Even the wind and sea obey him. Yet he
is a very present help in time of trouble (Psalm 46). God's people are
not exempt from the storms of life. Christian faith is not escapism. Just
prior to his great passion, Jesus reminded his disciples that they would
weep and lament and experience various tribulations (John 16:20,
33). Amid the storms, Jesus' presence does not fail. His love led him to
the cross. In that love he never forsakes his own. After this particular

incident, they were to learn that the Messiah who had chosen them to witness his mission would not permit them to perish (6:45–52).

Discussion:

1. Jesus Christ is Lord of the natural, physical and spiritual realms.

2. The word has power to convict of sin (law) and power to awaken repentance and faith (gospel).

3. Faithful use of the means of grace (word, absolution, sacraments) keeps disciples of the Messiah in close contact with him.

4. Parables must be read and interpreted within their own contextual setting.

CHAPTER FOUR

Contrasting Reactions to the Messiah's Ministry Mark 5:1–6:6

Jesus Gains a Witness 5:1–20

Mark provides a later evening setting (4:35) for another manifestation of messianic authority. Gerasa was a narrow strip on the eastern side of Lake Galilee. The territory was home to Gentiles and Jews. Limestone rock formations provided caves, some of which were used as tombs. People avoided the area because of Jewish burial taboos. Pervading superstitions marked that particular area as inhabited by demons.

It is a truly dramatic scene. The demoniac is both powerful and dangerous. In modern parlance he would be tagged a classic case of possession by another's will. The unclean spirit identifies itself as Legion. This is an undoubted reference to a Roman regiment of six thousand frequently stationed in the region. Mark stresses the unusual nature of this unusual case. Jesus "was saying" to the demon: Come out! Jesus "was asking" the demon's name. It is the intention of the Messiah that his disciples observe his full power and authority.

The unfolding drama rivets our attention upon two highly contrasting reactions to the Messiah's ministry. The Gerasenes, terrified by the antics of the crazed demoniac, seek to banish Jesus from their community. He had greatly disturbed their economy. The demoniac, now fully cleansed, clothed and clear of mind, begs to follow Jesus. He witnesses the good news throughout the essentially Greek cities of the district known collectively as Decapolis (1:14–15). Mark attests the universal nature of the gospel. It is truly for all. The mandate to proclaim the word in communities, which for centuries had boasted of their Greek culture and religion, is a powerful affirmation of the post-resurrection charge to preach the gospel to the entire world (16:15, 20).

Ministering to Human Need 5:21–43

Cures, healing and exorcisms may be classified as miracles. Many prefer to limit messianic miracles to restoring the dead to life. It is really a moot point. The Messiah's wondrous acts serve as witness to his authority and power. Restoring the dead to life is to be viewed as a special sign, which points to his own triumphant resurrection. The announcement at the tomb: He has risen. He is not here (16:6) validates his messianic commission.

The rule of the local synagogue is one of the most important members of the community. He literally throws himself at Jesus' feet as he begs the Lord to heal his dying daughter. On the way, Jesus is accosted by a woman with a stubborn gynecological malady. Mark labels it a scourge. Whatever the precise affliction, it affected both her physical and social well being. Her ceremonial uncleanness (Leviticus 15:25–27) virtually isolated her. Jesus praises her faith. He also speaks the welcome word of healing restoration.

Of special note are the words, which Jesus speaks to the distraught father. Do not fear! Only believe! Mourners had already assembled to render their sad, pathetic rites for the dead. They follow strict Jewish custom. The last thing they expect is a dramatic reversal. To their experience the finality of death is beyond appeal. They scornfully revile the suggestion that the girl is merely sleeping. Undaunted by this hard unbelief, Jesus speaks the word, which restores life. He vindicates the trust of Jairus.

Mark skillfully sketches contrasting responses to this ministry. On the one hand, there is no faith. On the other, there is great faith. We are confronted by despair and hope, rejection and reception, depths of distress and unbridled confidence. In particular, the grim reality of death surrenders to him who by his own death and resurrection steps before us as the conqueror of death.

The Messiah Encounters Painful Rejection 6:1–6

Compelling contrasts continue. Jesus has, at this point, achieved great popularity and recognition. Now he assumes the role of guest rabbi in Nazareth, in the very synagogue, which he had frequently attended. Here, among his own, he encounters only contempt and rejection. He must marvel at the unbelief, which acts as a restraint upon his healing ministry and desire to reach out in compassionate care. Mark alludes a second time to the biological family of Jesus (3:31–35). His humble lineage and vocation as a worker with wood apparently pose, at least in the minds of family and friends, obstacles to a messianic role. His own family obviously shares mistaken messianic notions, which over the centuries had obscured the nature of the kingdom of God. Their unbelief and prejudiced opposition simply amaze him. The statement about a prophet has become proverbial. Yet it has more than limited parochial significance. It is actually a verbal sign. It points to the confession of the church that Jesus Christ will come in glory to judge the living and the dead. The unbelief and rejection, which Jesus encounters in Nazareth of Galilee mirrors the unbelief and opposition of all who continue to be offended by his mission and message.

Discussion:

1. How does Jesus disturb people in every age? Why does he do so?
2. What alternatives present themselves when Jesus confronts people?
3. What is the real power of unbelief?
4. Death can conquer us or be conquered by us. All depends on relationship with Christ!

CHAPTER FIVE

The Messiah Does All Things Well
Mark 6:7–8:30

Messengers of the Messiah 6:7–34

In spite of rejection by his hometown, relatives and family, Jesus will not be silenced. He reacts by expanding his ministry. His disciples must learn that both failures and successes attend a calling through which he exercises his ministry after his resurrection and ascension (16:20). Jewish customs play an important role as Jesus commissions the twelve. Tunics were simple, coarsely woven inner garments. Sandals were removed as one entered a house. Wallets served personal needs, although cultists often used them to collect funds for their shrines and gods. Whenever a Jew entered courts of the Temple, he customarily laid aside staff, sandals and coin belt. This was to enable him to concentrate totally on worship.

Jesus assumes that his disciples will be accorded normal hospitality as they travel. If such is refused on account of the message they bring, they are to do what every Jew did upon leaving Gentile area. They are to shake off the unclean dust. They represent the Messiah. Their mission has highest priority. As they proclaim a message of judgment and grace, they are to show concern for the whole person. In the words of Psalm 45, God anointed his Messiah with the oil of gladness. Disciples of that Messiah are to anoint with the oil of healing.

Mark inserts into his account the tragic fate of an earlier messenger. John had carried out his ministry with faithfulness. Many debated whether he might actually be Elijah, returned from heaven to usher in the messianic kingdom. Others thought he might be a prophet like Moses. Herod Antipas had survived the murderous plots of his father to become puppet king over Galilee. Shallow, dissolute and totally vain, he had rebuked by John for his utter contempt of the law of God (Leviticus 18:16: 20:21). Herod spoke from the torments of a tortured conscience. On a sensual impulse, Herod had condemned the Baptizer to death. John lived and died for the truth he forcefully and fearlessly proclaimed. Jesus seeks that in his own disciples.

As the twelve report, Mark intentionally names them apostles, ones sent out on a mission. Demands on the Messiah increase as his popularity grows. Root cause of the continuing clamor for his ministry is not difficult to assess. People of his day were like sheep without loving, caring shepherds. Centuries before, God had proclaimed himself shepherd of Israel. He would lovingly guide and feed and protect his sheep, as his prophets would speak his word to them. Sadly, they often turned from their divine shepherd. Now the very human leaders of Israel had become false shepherds. The contrast, thought at the time veiled, is striking. Jesus had come to lay down his very life for the sheep. Apostles are his undershepherds. Their formidable task is to gather the lost sheep into the messianic fold known as the church.

Expanding Ministry

Feeding 5,000 is powerful testimony to a shepherd's compassionate concern. At the same time, it highlights a striking difference in the way Jesus and his disciples react to human need. As ambassadors of Christ, the disciples had brought spiritual and physical healing to those distressed in spirit and body. Now, on a late spring afternoon, they face a problem they would gladly avoid. They ask Jesus to dismiss the hungry crowd so that they may better tend to their own needs. Jesus does not share their callous attitude. Instead, he feeds the multitudes with overflowing abundance. The twelve had despaired of their own limited resources to meet the need. Now they are able to fill their baskets with fragments from the barley loaves and salt fish. They still have much to learn.

The Lord seeks the repose of the hills where he might pray and refresh his own body and spirit. At about 3 A.M., looking at a narrow point on the lake, he sees his disciples in trouble. Jesus approaches with assuring words: Take courage. Do not be afraid! His presence spells peace and calm, even though the disciples fail to comprehend the lessons he imparts. At Gennesareth, crowds once again surge upon Jesus. Is the Messiah merely being used by people who have no serious intention of responding to his call for repentance and faith? Regardless of their mindset, they are without hope and without a shepherd. Strengthened by prayer and a brief respite from the labors of the day, Jesus responds in compassionate concern as a good shepherd!

The Messiah and Tradition 7:1–23

In his narrative, Mark now shifts from the multitudes to persons of a totally different mind-set. Pharisees and others recognized as experts in Jewish law and tradition approach Jesus. To their religiously narrow point of view, Jesus and his disciples are guilty of an extremely serious infraction dealing with ritual uncleanness. What really is at issue is the authority of that body of rules, rites and regulations passed from one generation to another. Hebrew tradition is summarized in the Mishnah. Minutiae such as the proper amount water to be used, correct posture of hands, cleansing of cooking vessels and endless ritualistic taboos were intended to insure purity and devotion to God. Originally drawn from Leviticus 11–15, a greatly expanded tradition had, for many, become a substitute for divine law. In response, Jesus invokes the authority of one of the most revered prophets (Isaiah 29:13). His adversaries are hypocrites, actors posing as spiritual paragons as they play out roles with perfection and precision. Form, ritual, even tradition, may have a salutary place in devotion and worship. But they must never replace worship in spirit and in truth.

In their misguided zeal for ceremonial correctness, those who accuse the Messiah of flagrant misdeed have, in reality, abandoned the word of God. Their practice of Korban is a specific example. God's holy law specifies honor and care for parents. Both Pharisees and scribes claim to uphold that law. Yet they refuse to honor and support parents by a very clever ploy. They dedicate money and possessions to God and Temple without actually parting with either. Love remains the greatest of all commandments. They abrogate that by their selfish devices. Jesus drives home an important lesson. Defilement before God is not a matter of external acts.

Acceptance in the sight of God is not achieved by observing elaborate ceremonial rituals. An unregenerate heart despoils a human being. An untamed will spawns desires and choices such as forms of immorality, insolent self-centeredness and arrogance, hatred and pride. These are contrary to the express will of God. A new will, created by God and bestowed upon one as a gift of grace, redirects human desires and actions. These words of Jesus constitute a hard and sweeping dictum, so radical that his own disciples cannot at the time handle it. Jesus must destroy any system, as well meaning as it may be, which dishonors God and makes true repentance and faith possible.

Commendation, Confession and Conclusion 7: 24:8:30

Mark draws his account of the Galilean ministry to a close. He recounts how Jesus travels to Phoenicia on his return to the Decapolis. In that day, Tyre and Sidon were Gentile lands, even though the region was originally assigned to the tribe of Asher (Joshua 19:28–29). To Jews, Gentiles were unclean people, their houses unclean dwellings, their cities unclean territory. Jesus' action may serve as a symbol of the precious discussion. His popularity among the masses is nearing its peak. Yet his king and spiritual leaders have all but rejected his ministry. That has become an occasion for ministry to Gentiles, a decisive sign of things to come (16:15–16).

The incident involving the Syrophoenician woman at first hearing appears to cast Jesus in an unsympathetic role. Dogs were not humans' best friends. Gentiles considered the term, dog, an utterly contemptuous epithet. Jews, not unexpectantly, thought the term eminently appropriate for Gentiles. Jesus uses the diminutive form of the word to refer to house pets. The Messiah has come to his own people, Israel. The woman is fully aware of that. She does not argue the point. But he is Savior of all. Her faith clings to that. Her earnest prayer is answered.

The trip must have taken several weeks, during which Jesus undoubtedly prepared his disciples for what was to be a critical and crucial moment (8:27–29). The man brought to him has a particularly vexing problem. He is not only deaf; he has some impediment of speech. Jesus does not treat him as a file number in a therapy center. He is an individual in dire need. Looking heavenward, a sign of Hebrew piety and prayer (Psalm 121:1), Jesus audibly groans as with other symbolic actions he heals. Amazed, the crowds give this significant witness to Messiah's ministry: He has done all things well! The same verdict was spoken by God in his creation (Genesis 1:31). The new creation, the messianic age, has dawned in the person and ministry of Jesus (1:10–11, 14–15).

Jesus is no stranger to the district of ten cities known as Decapolis.

Some who gather about him may be present as a direct result of the testimony of the cured demoniac (5:1–20). Again, Jesus responds to physical need as he feeds four thousand. On this occasion, baskets used to gather fragments are not those in which Jews carried food. Gentiles used them. Things are moving too fast for Jesus' adversaries. Unable to comprehend the staggering truth that the Messiah provides for all, they request signs of affirmation. Such requests are nothing new. They are symptomatic of any age in which the message of God's acting in Christ for our salvation seems too dull, too banal, too ordinary or too radical. Jesus has provided ample signs. The eyes of Pharisees and their spiritual kin, like those of the blind man of Bethsaida, remain closed. His own disciples are slow to perceive (Jeremiah 5:21) because they are preoccupied with other matters. Jesus is divinely patient. Like the blind man, the disciples gradually attain clear vision. For they recognize and openly confess that Jesus is God's anointed servant.

Bethsaida was home to Peter, Andrew and Philip. Excavations have uncovered houses of fishermen dating from early New Testament times. Caesarea Philippi, the city in which the climatic confession of the disciples is witnessed, was situated at the northern end of the Jordan River Valley. It was built by another of Herod's (the Great) sons, who dedicated it, along with its magnificent white temple, to the honor and veneration of the Roman emperor. Its great harbor was constructed B.C. 22–10. Foundation of its lighthouse has been uncovered. Later in the history of the early church, cruel persecutions were launched because Christians refused to acknowledge the divinity of Caesar or the Roman state. They confessed boldly that Jesus alone is Lord of all lords and King of all kings. Many who refused to compromise their confession paid the ultimate price of sacrifice. They were ready to die for the Messiah who had died – and risen – for them.

Discussion:

1. The New Testament church sees in Psalm 23 a reference to Jesus as a good and true shepherd.

2. One does not become sinful by sinning. One sins because one is sinful.

3. Legalism centers in external acts. Christian life is motivated by the gospel and internal impulses.

Conclusion

Mark has crafted his narrative with extreme care. His account of the early ministry of Jesus leads step by step to the peak of the Messiah's power and popularity. Mark records healings, exorcisms, taming of elements, feeding of multitudes, forgiving of sins and astounding deeds, which serve to attract hordes of people. Amazed and astonished, they react to this ministry by expressing the judgment: He has done all things well! This is preparatory to the grand declaration made by the apostles: You are the Christ! At this juncture in the narrative we are, in a sense, back where we began. He who is acclaimed by his disciples to be the Messiah is the one who at his baptism is attested by the Holy Spirit to be Son of God. This good news unfolds in his preaching, teaching and healing ministry.

The church, which has always found it necessary clearly to define her beliefs, learned well form the witness carefully recorded by Mark (and other New Testament writers). Jesus of Nazareth is Son of God (1:1,11; 9:7; 15:39), Messiah (8:29; 14:61), Savior (10:45) who comes in the name of Yahweh (11:9), son of David (12:35), King of the Hews (15:26) and risen Lord (16:6) who sits at the right hand of the Father (16:19). Statements of faith framed by the church are known as creeds and confessions. By far the best known is the Apostles' Creed, so named because it expresses apostolic faith and teaching. It has long stood as a primary witness to Christian beliefs. The earliest version of this creed developed out of the baptismal confession made by news converts. Present form of the creed dates roughly from the eighth century.

The Nicene Creed is named after the city in Asia Minor where an assembly of church leaders met in A.D. 325. It was framed as an orthodox (right-teaching) expression of the Christian Faith, several articles of which had been in contention. Slightly modified by another Council in 381, it was reaffirmed as the basic creed of the church in 451. It delineates the nature of God as triune and explicitly distinguishes the person and works of Father, Son and Holy Spirit.

Third of the chief confessions is named in honor of Athanasius, stalwart defender of orthodox teaching in the fourth century. Though of uncertain origin, it claims to present the Christian Faith whole and undefiled and summons one to believe it firmly and faithfully for salvation.

Part Two

Suffering and Tragedy

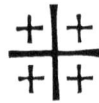

+|+
+|+

CHAPTER SIX

Predictions of the Passion
Mark 8:31–10:52

Losing and Gaining Life 8:31–9:1

Reflect for a moment on the structure of this particular Gospel. The early period of messianic ministry is one of increasing popularity and power. At the same time, rumblings of firm opposition gain intensity. They finally culminate in the tragedy whose climax is betrayal, abandonment and crucifixion. Mark introduces this perceptible shift as he recounts the first explicit reference to suffering, rejection and death. A motif of tragedy replaces a motif of power. Allusions to the Messiah's impending passion increase, while his popularity decreases. Opposition to his ministry increases, while his amazing works markedly decrease.

Mark records three predictions of the Messiah's suffering and death (8:31; 9:31; 10:33). The first provokes opposition from the disciples. Peter confesses Jesus to be Christ. Now Peter rebukes him whom he has just confessed! In doing so, Peter assumes the role of spokesman for Satan. Peter insists that Jesus forge a different path for himself. In Peter's mind, the time is ripe to step forward and lay claim to David's throne. Then Jesus can easily enlist multitudes that have followed him, launch a mighty crusade to destroy the idols of the Gentiles and exalt the name of Yahweh among his liberated people. So away with talk of suffering and death! Peter is actually reprising the great testing in the wilderness. At the very beginning of the Messiah's ministry, Satan had sought to derail his entire mission (1:12–13). Now sadly misguided and confused, disciples want to foist their own agenda upon the Lord.

Jesus strongly rebukes the rebuker. He and the others have so much to learn. True discipleship does not consist in advising their Master. It involves opposition, self-denial, suffering, even death for the sake of the gospel. It summons to bold confession of Jesus in a world turned

in upon its own pleasures, popularity and profit. Jesus' path will ultimately lead to the right kind of glory. Those who follow his path will
experience similar glory.

A Glimpse of Glory 9:2–13

A week following the unqualified confession at Caesarea Philippi
(8:27–29), the so-called inner circle of apostles is afforded an unforgettable confirmation of faith. Once again, Mark shows himself to be
a capable and imaginative writer. He introduces Jesus as Messiah and
Son of God (1:1–13). Then Mark portrays the Messiah's ministry,
which elicits the confession of the twelve (8:29), provides a glimpse
of the Messiah-Son in his transfiguration (9:7–8), records the witness
of the Roman centurion (15:39) and reports the fulfillment of the
Messiah's prediction of resurrection (16:1–8).

High on Mt. Hermon, Jesus experiences a temporary metamorphosis.
The incident is enriched by several well-known Old Testament allusions (Exodus 19:9; 34:29; 40:34; Deuteronomy 18:15). Moses was
mediator of Torah, literally, instruction in God's ways. Elijah was revered as greatest of the prophets of Yahweh. Their presence symbolizes the divine truth that the ministry of Jesus fulfills the law and the
prophets. The glistening radiance, cloud and voice reassure Jesus that
he is indeed the chosen of God. The very same heavenly phenomena
reassure bewildered apostles that Jesus is God's Messiah whether he
fits their preconceived notions or not. The brightness of the mount
also provides a vivid image to which they can cling when the awful
darkness of Good Friday overwhelms them. The glimpse of glory additionally prepares them to witness the gospel in and to a world, which
turns in on its own spiritual darkness and ignorance. As they return to
the plain, Jesus furnishes another powerful sign of messiahship. Jewish
lore spoke of Elijah's return to announce the advent of God's reign. Jesus reveals that Elijah has come in the person of John (Malachi 4:5–6).
As the disciples recall what happened to John, they are to realize the
fate, which awaits their master.

Belief and Unbelief 9:14–50

Coming down from a mountaintop experience is always difficult
and deflating. Peter desires to prolong the glory. Erecting booths

or tabernacles is an obvious reference to the Hebrew Feast of Tabernacles, which commemorates the sojourns of Israel following the Exodus. Meanwhile, other disciples face an embarrassing and unsolvable impasse. They had cast out demons (6:12–13). Facing an aggravating case of epilepsy, they appear to be helpless and powerless. Jesus uses the occasion to contrast belief (of the father) with unbelief (of the multitudes). In that context, he takes charge of the situation. He performs one of the three recorded healings, which occur after his prediction of his passion. The root cause of the disciples' inability to heal was lack of prayer. They had power. They had failed to nurture it.

Jesus undertakes what proves to be his final trip through Galilee on the way to Jerusalem. He continues to prepare his disciples. The Son of Man is being delivered into the hands of those who will kill him. But he will rise from the dead. Those closest to him once again fail to comprehend. Perhaps their spiritual perception is blurred by visions of their own importance. They are fashioning a role for themselves in a national, political kingdom, which they expect to be established. Jesus injects a powerful pictorial lesson. Powerless little children have a greater place in his kingdom that powers brokers. Furthermore, his disciples do not have an exclusivist curb on messianic power and privilege. In highly metaphorical and vivid terms, Jesus insists that the kingdom -embodied in his mission - calls for sacrifice, discipline, self-denial and service. Greatness does not lie in endless disputes about how to be great! It consists in serving. Disciples are to be like salt. Salt was a highly valued commodity. It was employed in sacrifice, as a symbol of purification and as a seasoning preservative. Lives offered in service to Jesus purify, season and preserve a society, which is basically self-serving, self-glorifying and self-perpetuating. In brief, a life filled with Christ and dedicated to Christ bespeaks faith in Christ. Any other stands as a testimony to unbelief and separation from Christ.

Entangled and Tested 10:1–31

Storm clouds mass over the Messiah's ministry. Mark relates several incidents that lead Jesus to hostile confrontation with his adversaries and disagreement with his disciples. Pharisees seek to entangle him in the volatile question of divorce — a seemly innocent query — but whatever answer Jesus might give can snare him into nasty controversy with major rabbinical schools of interpretation, with Herod who had unlawfully put away his wife (6:16–19) and with the supreme council (Sanhedrin), which dictated rules of divorce. Jesus cites the Mosaic code spelled out in Deuteronomy 24:11. This was usually accorded liberal interpretation in Jesus' time. Jesus grounds his position in the creation account of Genesis 1:27 and 2:24. By so doing, he avoids possible entanglement with his enemies and reaffirms the sacred relationship of marriage.

The next incident invited another rebuke from the disciples. Mothers traditionally sought out rabbis to bless their children. The disciples rebuke those bringing them and, indirectly, Jesus for receiving them. He uses the occasion to describe the nature of the messianic kingdom. Childlike (not childish) faith in the gospel for entrance into God's kingdom is an absolute prerequisite on the part of people of all ages. In its context, the passage does not treat Christian baptism. Nevertheless, the Church has long used it, as she reaches out in the Savior's name to touch children with his grace.

Dialog with the wealthy young man tests Jesus' understanding of the force of Torah as moral law. Jesus first clears the air of all pretenses. He recites commandments, which treat interpersonal relationships. The young man is obviously deeply sincere. Convinced that Jesus can answer his crucial question, he responds with the confidence of a seasoned practitioner of the Mosaic code. In equally sincere love, Jesus lays bare a fatal flaw in the man's spiritual makeup. His problem is not that he is rich or that he is young. His heart is not right with God. He loves treasures more than the life he claims to be seeking. He values gold more than God's grace. That is always a barrier to eternal life. Salvation is God's gift. It cannot be purchased with morality, money or a mind, which asks what one must do to save oneself.

Peter is quick to form a personal judgment. The disciples have forsaken much to follow Jesus. Isn't there some kind of reward for such obedience? Denial for the sake of the gospel, replies Jesus, is always recognized. But it is not always rewarded in this life, nor in the way some would choose. It may even include persecution. God is the judge of that. Those who use spiritual computers to tally worth in the sight of God might end up last in line instead of first. And if they forget that the God of grace rewards out of grace, they may even sadly discover that they are not in line at all!

Serving to Save 10:32–52

Mark points to Jerusalem and the tragedy waiting to be played out there. The city of peace is to become the locale of betrayal, abandonment and crucifixion. At first Jesus walks alone. He no doubt ponders the way of sorrows (Via Dolorosa) he must walk alone. His disciples are both bewildered and fearful. The third and final prediction of the passion is more detailed than the others (8:31; 9:31). That assists us in trying to fathom the confusion of the twelve. They have confessed that Jesus is the Messiah. They find it difficult, if not virtually impossible, to understand why Jesus is going to Jerusalem to die. The request of James and John reveals something of the nature of their confusion. Jesus is impelled by servant hood. That leads to the way of the cross. His disciples are impelled by visions of power, status, and prestige. That leads to a decidedly different way. They also seek concrete evidence of the benefits derived from following him.

Their request is not clothed with subtle innuendo. Do for us whatever we ask you! It is about as neat a package as one could possibly request. And one that entangles Jesus is a bitter in-house squabble. Ambition in religion can be just as sinful, manipulative and exploitive as any other kind of ambition. The fact that these two brothers had been invited into the inner circle of disciples further suggests that they even expected preferential treatment above the others.

Jesus is a master of parable. He is equally a master of metaphor. In Hebrew thought, the cup (or chalice) depicts one's lot or destiny (Psalms 23:5; 75:8). A baptism is being submerged in a particularly overwhelming experience (Psalms 42:7; 69:2). The Messiah's cup and baptism are to suffer and die as God's chosen servant (Isaiah 53) to redeem and save humankind. If the disciples would only realize that they would no longer be arguing about rank and honor in his kingdom.

Mark relates a final incident, which occurs prior to Jesus' entry into Jerusalem. It graphically highlights four critical and important truths: 1) Jesus' compassion is not diminished by his preoccupation with the trials he will encounter within the week. Many seek to silence Bartimaeus. Jesus responds to the blind beggar's anguished cry for mercy. 2) The man clothes his confession of faith in a messianic formula. It is echoed in the chant of the Palm Sunday crowds. The title, Son of David, was overlaid with a number of ambiguous political nuances. Yet it expressed the hope of many that God's Messiah would be a spiritual deliverer (Isaiah 61:1–3; 35:3–6). 3) The blindness of Bartimaeus symbolizes the spiritual blindness of the apostles. They still cannot comprehend the mission of Jesus in terms of fulfillment of God's purposes and promises. 4) As Bartimaeus receives physical sight and follows the Lord, so the disciples finally gain spiritual sight and follow the risen Christ who continues his ministry though their word and witness.

Discussion:

1. Spiritual misconceptions often get in the way of proper understanding of God.

2. Religion can be a cloak for ruthless self-centeredness.

3. Why are we tempted to think that our ways are better than God's ways?

Confrontation and Controversy
Mark 11:1–12:44

The Messiah Comes to His Temple 11:1–21

The main road into Jerusalem took the traveler through Jericho. The ancient village was situated about fifteen miles northeast of Jerusalem. It was known in Hebrew lore as the city whose walls had fallen at trumpets' blast (Joshua 6). A number of part-time priests who served in the temple lived in Jericho. Some had quite likely made up part of the crowd, which witnessed the healing of Bartimaeus. Bethphage (house of figs) offered lodging for pilgrims overflowing the accommodations to be had in Jerusalem. For the temple attracted thousands of worshippers, especially during the major Jewish festivals.

Jesus enters the holy city surrounded by crowds who customarily accompanied a teacher. He had enjoined silence on those who witnessed his messianic deeds. Now the time for silence is over. He accepts the acclaim accorded him as the Coming One, a title easily recognized as a name for Yahweh's Messiah. The excited multitudes cry out to heaven: Save us, O God. The Messiah has come. Save us now! (Psalm 118:26). Mark appends a significant comment. As Jesus later goes to the temple, the milling multitudes are gone. He is alone. It is a provocative portent of the events of the week just begun. At its end he will be totally alone. Israel's Messiah will be abandoned by its leaders, by his own disciples, and even by his God (15:34). Finally he will lie alone in a borrowed tomb (15:46).

In the sacred precincts of the temple was the courts especially designated for Gentiles. It was separate from the temple proper, which was known as the Court of the Priests. There the Messiah enters into direct confrontation with Sadducees, as well as scribes, both experts in the Law of Moses. Sadducees were for the most part aristocratic and wealthy. They were also politically astute. They worked in concert with the Roman authorities. Rome, in turn, respected their authority in the temple and in matters of Jewish religious customs. Jews were required to pay an annual tax in shekels for the upkeep of their major house of worship. Money exchange in the outer courts of the temple was a matter of convenience. Doves were used for sacrifice (Leviticus 12:8; 14:22). Jesus' anger is directed at the exploitation permitted by the chief priests and at the disrespect shown to the temple, his Father's house. A place holy to God had become an unholy den of robbers (Isaiah 56:7). The statement is quite possibly an allusion to thieves who frequented caves found on the road from Jerusalem to Jericho. The Messiah's challenge to priestly authority is overtly clear. Priestly reaction to his challenge is equally clear and overt. The religious leaders of Israel plot to kill him.

Questions of Authority 11:22–12:34

Jesus deliberately enters the arena of controversy with those who oppose his ministry. The die is cast. The mission that lies before him will be extremely difficult. His resource is prayer. His practice of prayer provides an impressive example (14:32–42). Jewish rabbis often spoke of seemingly insurmountable difficulties as mountains that must be removed. Jesus instructs his disciples that such can happen. The power of faith-supported prayer, offered in a spirit of confidence and an attitude of loving forgiveness, is the means for doing so.

While in the temple, Jesus is accosted by representatives of the supreme religious council of Israel known as the Sanhedrin. At issue is the sensitive question of authority. Where does Jesus derive his authority to drive from the temple those who, to his mind, were profaning its sacred area? And whence is his authority to teach in its cloisters, or covered porches? The deputation of priests, scribes and elders seek to entrap him in a sticky theological dilemma. If he insists that he is acting on his own authority they will arrest him as a dangerous heretic for he is defying their spiritual authority. If he claims to be acting on God's behalf, they will accuse him of blasphemy. In either case, he will no longer pose a threat to their authority and power.

The counter question framed by Jesus places them on the sharp horns of a dilemma. What about the baptism performed by John? Was it of God? If so, why had they vehemently opposed it? If they maintain that it was purely John's own invention they will incur the wrath of the people for they considered John to be a heroic martyr who suffered at the hands of the weak, self-indulgent king. The deputation stumbles upon its own vaunted pretensions. Jesus then drives his point home by means of a penetrating parable. God planted his vineyard, Israel (Isaiah 5:1–7). Cultivators of the vineyard are its religious leaders, the very ones who are challenging Jesus' ministry. Servants are the prophets whom God sent to his people. The son and heir is God's own Messiah. Jesus then turns the metaphor. He cites Psalm 118:22–23. Those commissioned to care for God's people are even now rejecting him who is the keystone of the arch that holds the spiritual temple together. Early Christians and New Testament writers found in this application of the Psalm a clear reference to the church, which is built upon the death and resurrection of Christ.

Next in line to entrap Jesus are Pharisees and Herodians, unnatural and uneasy allies who had already put aside their differences in order to plot his death (3:6). Approaching him with sycophantic flattery, they attempt to snare him in a highly flammable political dilemma. The imperial government imposed three kinds of taxes on Jews. Least burdensome was the so-called personal tax, which amounted to a denarius, a small silver Roman coin. The scenario is complex. First, a prerogative of government is the authority to levy taxes. The Roman Empire had achieved great proficiency in exercising this broad power. Second, coinage in the Empire served as a symbol of that authority. That small denarius proclaimed two things, which were totally abhorrent to Jews. The image of Caesar (in this instance that of Tiberius, adopted son and successor of Augustus) declared his ultimate political authority over Israel. The reverse side of the coin proclaimed him, a pagan, to be the supreme religious authority over the whole Empire.

The plan to put Jesus in an impossible situation is truly ingenious. If he opposes taxes, he will be openly denounced as a Zealot and revolutionary in rebellion against Rome. If he affirms taxes, he will be openly denounced as a renegade rebel against Israel. His adversaries are stunned by his answer. He recognizes spheres of spiritual and secular authority, declaring that people are subject to both.

Status seeking Sadducees have no desire to get involved in political controversy, especially one involving Caesar. So they deftly turn to a theological question. It deals with a disputed doctrine. Sadducees reject the notion of resurrection, claiming that it is not taught in the Pentateuch (five scrolls or books of Moses). Pharisees accept and teach the doctrine. Now it is used to question Jesus' authority to interpret the Old Testament. First, they ignore the real purpose of levirate marriage taught in Deuteronomy 25:5–10. This was to assure family and property rights. Next they cleverly put forth a hypothesis that will surely trap Jesus. At best, a response will pit him against all Pharisees. At worst, a response will make him out to be a theological simpleton. Jesus handles both their impudence and their improbable hypothesis with unexpected skill. You are dead wrong, replies Jesus. You do not know the very Scriptures you claim to respect. You do not understand the power of God! There is a resurrection. There is life after physical death. The God of the patriarchs is the God of the living, not of the dead.

Note how carefully and capably Mark leads his readers to examine the authority of Christ. First, there is his personal authority to cleanse the temple and to teach. Second, there is his firm judgment regarding political authority. Third, there is the exercise of theological authority. At the peak of this literary crescendo, Mark now relates the interchange between Jesus and a scribe. It goes to the very heart and core of the Old Testament religion. Jesus recites Shema, the creed of Israel found in Deuteronomy 6:4. (See also 6:4–9, 11:13–21.) With it Jesus combines Leviticus 19:18, expanding it to include all humankind. The scribe's question could have involved Jesus in a no-win rabbinical controversy. The Messiah's answer is commended by the scribe whom Jesus in turn commends to the kingdom of God.

Religion Put To The Test 12:35–44

Jesus now picks up the important theme sounded by the blind man of Jericho (10:46–52) and resounded by the crowds of Palm Sunday (11:7–10). Is God's Anointed One correctly identified as Son of David, the popular king of Israel? Scribes long considered Psalm 110:1 to be of Davidic authorship and of messianic content. Jesus cites the passage. The Messiah is indeed a descendant of David. But if David, moved by the Holy Spirit, calls the Messiah his Lord then the Messiah must be more than a mere human being who can claim descent from a royal line! The title, Son of David, is to be viewed in its total context.

It must be viewed primarily as a spiritual concept, not as a revolutionary cry for action. Once again, messianic theology is being tested. But more is at stake. The very practice of religion is being put to the test. Scribes may be experts in the proper exercise of religion. At the same time, they cheat widows! The needy widow's meager contribution of two small copper coins (lepton) worth less than a penny represents genuine sacrifice on her part. She willingly gives for the upkeep of the temple. She is motivated by love to surrender all she had to live on to God. Her practice of religion gains both approval and approbation.

The Messiah will now leave his temple. His last moments there are spent in the so-called court of women where offering receptacles were placed. His teaching ministry is about to end. His passion is about to begin. His enemies have failed to ensnare him with their cleverly and deviously concocted questions. They embark upon another curse – one predicted by Jesus – which will accomplish their goal once and for all. They intensify their plans to plot his death.

Discussion:

1. Palm Sunday multitudes acclaim Jesus as the Messiah. But what it their understanding of it?

2. Is there a difference between these two phrases: David said in the Holy Spirit, and, every Scripture is inspired?

3. Jewish rabbis and commentators sometimes claimed that God gave six hundred and thirteen laws on Sinai. St. Augustine (354–430) claims there is only one: Love God and do as you desire! Is this adequate for the Christian life?

4. Religion in itself is neither a blessing nor a curse. What makes either?

CHAPTER EIGHT

Warnings and Prophecies
Mark 13:1–37

Mark has recorded three prophetic announcements of the Messiah's rejection, sufferings, death and resurrection. After the first prediction, Mark appends the words of Jesus in which he states that some will not die until they see the kingdom of God come with power (9:1). In this section of his Gospel, Mark records similar words uttered by Jesus (13:30). Both statements belong, in a broad sense, to what is known as apocalyptic discourse. Apocalyptic literally denotes an unveiling or uncovering. It is a revelation, a making known, of things which are to occur. The entire collection of warnings and prophecies narrated by Mark (13:1–37) is often titled, The Little Apocalypse. The last book of the New Testament bears the superscription, Apocalypse of John. More accurately stated, it is the Apocalypse of Jesus Christ to his servant John. This servant speaks to the churches of Asia Minor for the greater part in highly symbolic and picturesque visions. Numbers, colors, personages, places, names and images are all codes to veiled meaning.

At the end of the first Christian century an Apocalypse, or Revelation, was composed by a certain Hermas. It is known as the Shepherd of Hermas and contains visions, warnings of dire persecutions, parables and even commandments. It exerted great influence upon the early church even though it did not gain admittance into the New Testament Canon. In the second and third centuries a number of such Apocalypses were composed in the name of apostles. Best known may be that attributed to Peter. It graphically and meticulously describes the punishments of the damned in hell.

Apocalypticism in general deals with catastrophic cosmic events. Its literature portrays conflicts between good and evil, divine judgments and the struggles of God's people against satanic powers. Great emphasis is usually placed on the irruption into human history of what is referred to as a great Day of the Lord (Isaiah 13:6–10). This ushers in a new age. At the time of Jesus, a vast and rich store of Jewish apocalyptic literature had been amassed. Some has roots in Old Testament imagery drawn primarily from Ezekiel, Daniel and Zechariah. The book of Joel, e.g., provides the text (2:28–32) for the first Christian sermon recorded in the New Testament (Acts 2:17–21). Some of the literature popular in the first century traces its origins to the dreams, visions, hopes, faith, aspirations, frustrations and fears of Israel as its people wondered and waited for the Day of the Lord to dawn. Jesus weaves a number of strands of apocalyptic into his discourse on destruction, persecution, dangers and warnings. He does this as he is invited to respond to the wonderment and curiosity of his disciples.

Dangers

The temple is closely associated with the closing days of the Messiah's ministry. Now it becomes the locus and focus of his commentary on things to come. The temple was a truly magnificent structure, the showplace of Jerusalem. It was known as Herod's temple because reconstruction had begun about 20 B.C. during the reign of Herod the Great. It boasted massive walls, pillars, stones and colonnades. Actually, it was a complex of several buildings. The inner part was a particularly impressive masterpiece of architectural design. In the discussion with his disciples, Jesus foretells its complete and utter destruction. This occurred in A.D. 70. Exact date of seizure of the temple is set as September 8. After a horrible siege of Jerusalem, during which the hated Roman symbol was planted at the eastern gate of the temple and pagan sacrifices were offered, Roman General Titus ruthlessly razed the temple complex. Jesus employs apocalyptic found in Daniel (9:7; 11:31–35; 112:11) to depict the profanation of the house of God. His hearers were well acquainted with the abomination that took place in 168 B.C.. Syrian ruler, Antiochius IV, known as Epiphanes pillaged the temple and set up a pagan altar in its holy place. Some sixty years after the event of A.D. 70, Jerusalem was rebuilt as a pagan, Roman city. It was even renamed.

Other perils confront the Messiah's disciples. They are to expect persecution. It will come from Jewish leaders and from Gentile rulers. It will split families and stir the hatred of closest friends (see Micah 7:5–7). Confounding the confusion and chaos will be the appearance of false messiahs. Charlatan prophets will perform great signs as they claim to speak for Jesus. Such tribulations will, however, become an avenue for Spirit-filled witness to the gospel, which is to be proclaimed among all the nations. Those who faithfully endure are assured of salvation.

Warnings

Jesus employs vivid imagery, found in Daniel (7:13–14), of the Son of Man. The Messiah will most certainly return. He will come in great glory. His return is preceded by fearsome natural, cosmic and political upheavals. The lesson imparted is direct and pointed. Watch! All things will ultimately pass away, not just the temple. But the Messiah's words will never pass away. Cling to them! The Day of the Lord will be a day of judgment. But it will be a day of deliverance as well. Jesus also makes it clear that no one knows when the Lord will return, no one! Only the Father knows that. Any who claim such knowledge, by special revelation or privileged information, are false teachers. Do not listen to them. When the Lord does come you will know it. Those who are watching and waiting in firm faith and confidence will greet him as the Messiah, Savior and Lord.

Discussion:

1. How does the canon of the Scripture differ from non-canonical or apocryphal books?

2. What are signs of a false prophet? How can one recognize false messiahs?

3. Those who purport to know date and time of Christ's return contradict the clear word of God.

4. Watch and pray. This is how we prepare for the coming of the Lord.

CHAPTER NINE

Betrayal and Crucifixion
Mark 14:15–47

Preparation 14:1–16

With brevity, precision and thoroughness Mark sets the stage for final
scenes of the drama, which lead to the Messiah's total abandonment.
Mark introduces the series of events by carefully fixing both time and
place. Passover was one of the three major Jewish festivals. It was observed 14 Nisan (roughly April) and was immediately followed by a
seven-day celebration known as the Feast of Unleavened Bread (Exodus 12). Rome was always wary of Passover. Ancient accounts of freedom kindled anew the desire on the part of Israel to shed the political
yoke imposed by a foreign and pagan power. Adult males were expected to participate in the festival. Remembrance of God's deliverance
of their fathers from the bondage of Egypt was so compelling that it
prompted others to come as well.

Some estimate that as many as a million pilgrims might converge upon
Jerusalem at any given Passover. The Roman governor, whose resi-
dence was normally in Caesarea Philippi, usually moved to Jerusalem
in order to keep a close eye on the festival and the mood of the people.
Jewish authorities were also alert to problems that might arise. Priests
and scribes are determined to arrest Jesus and condemn him. But they
realize full well that explosive tensions can easily get out of hand. They
want to avoid any overt act, which might serve as pretext for intervention by Roman garrisons conveniently quartered in an armory close to
the temple.

Events leading to the inevitability of the cross move swiftly. In Jerusalem, the Messiah's enemies plot to destroy him. In nearby Bethany, an
unnamed woman anoints Jesus with a rare and expensive nard. Jesus
praises her unusual act of devotion as a sign of his impending death
and burial. Meanwhile, one of his disciples offers to betray him to
those plotting his arrest.

On the first day of the feast, Jesus dispatches two disciples to Jerusalem. Their task is to prepare for the Passover ritual and meal. Preparations were elaborate. All leaven must be removed from the house. The lamb must be purchased, sacrificed in the temple and roasted. Unleavened bread, salt, water, various herbs, fruits, cinnamon and wine must be procured. Jesus acts as host. He will conduct the Passover liturgy.

The Final Passover 14:17–26

The next scene of the drama opens after 6 pm. This marks the beginning of the Hebrew day. The Messiah and his disciples begin the age-old fellowship and commemorative meal. Their spiritual oneness is suddenly shattered. Jesus reveals the sad truth of treachery. The betrayer is not an outsider, not a hanger-on, not a casual acquaintance, not a renegade religionist, not a misguided zealot, not a disillusioned former disciple, not a declared enemy. The betrayer is one of his own, one who is at meal with him. Grieved by the startling announcement, the disciples respond one by one with denials. Is Jesus offering a final warning? There is still time for Judas from Iscaroth (3:19) to repent his action. There is still time to receive forgiveness, which is offered in the gospel for all to seek and claim. Passover rituals were exacting in their requirements. Mark does not intend to provide elaborate details of the service of remembrance and thanksgiving. Rather he emphasizes what is new and totally different in this particular one.

As they are eating, Jesus, serving as host, follows the tradition. He blesses the load as he blesses the Lord God, King of the universe, for providing bread for his people. He breaks the bread, normally eaten as a reminder of the bread of affliction eaten by their forefather slaves in Egypt. But as he distributes it he bids his disciples to take it as his own body. Four cups of wine are prescribed for the meal. The first is named Kiddush, or sanctification. It separates Passover from a common meal. The second is called proclamation. The third is the cup of thanksgiving. Over it a blessing is spoken praising God for the gift of the fruit of the vine. Jesus most likely takes this cup and gives it to the disciples as the blood of the new covenant (testament) being shed for many. The fourth and last cup is drunk as the assembly sings Psalm 136 and concluding prayers are offered. At this commemoration of the old covenant, God's Messiah establishes both a new covenant and a new feast. It is based neither on law nor remembrance of God's great acts of the past. Jesus bases it on the gospel and the inauguration of the kingdom of God (1:14–15). The final prayer of the Passover liturgy praises God as King. It confesses that beside you, O Lord, we have no King, no Redeemer and no Savior. The church continues to celebrate the meal of remembrance, fellowship, thanksgiving (eucharist) and praise as Christ's own receive his body and blood for the assurance of grace proclaimed in the gospel.

Abandonment 14:27–15:20

Predictions of the Lord's Passion (8:31; 9:31; 10:33) are about to find a sad fulfillment. The Messiah will die. But he will be raised to life. In this next dramatic scene, Mark portrays what might be called the night of abandonment. Rich symbolism heightens one's awareness of the tragic reality. For darkness has taken over. From the Passover chamber to Gethsemane's garden and trial before the supreme council, to the High Priest's house and to the bugle call (gallicinium: cock-crow) at 3 am, all the players are acting out their roles covered by the darkness of night. Under the cloak of darkness priests and leaders of Israel abandon Jesus to their fears and insecurities. Leaders and disciples are stripped bare of every pretense of flattery (12:13–14) and of every avowal of faithfulness (14:27–31). Mark finally provides a fitting symbol in the youth (possibly Mark himself) who speeds naked thought the night to safety.

In the light of the new day the Sanhedrin reassembles. In the preceding hours of darkness, the hastily summoned supreme council of seventy-one had accused Jesus of the capital crime of blasphemy. He admitted his claim to be God's Messiah, Son of God and Son of Man who will be enthroned at God's right hand of majesty and come in heavenly glory. The council had violated its own rules against meeting at night and at a chief festival. That did not concern these religionists who were determined to maintain their power and authority. However, they do lack power under Roman jurisdiction to carry out their purpose and sentence. Pontius Pilate, personal representative of the emperor, must authorize execution. Blasphemy against the God of Israel is not a crime against Rome. Treason is. Any hint that Jesus wants to be a king or that he questions the payment of taxes to Caesar would gain the attention of the procurator.

Pilate is shrewd enough and experienced enough to recognize that religious respectability is the cloak worn by the Sanhedrin to cover its malicious hatred of Jesus. The political accusation is nothing more than one of convenience. Pilate evades making the judgment only he could legally hand down. He offers the crowd a choice. Do they want him to release a convicted rebel or one called King of the Jews? The people bow to the desires of their religious leaders. They abandon Jesus to their fanatical folly. Jesus is handed over to unrestrained scourging and mockery.

Cross and Burial 15:21–47

With characteristic directness, Mark takes us to Golgotha, the mound outside Jerusalem's gates where crucifixions were routinely carried out. A cross of wood in the shape of a T (the Tau cross) is prepared by the military detail. The cross was normally carried to the site of execution by the prisoner. Mark does not elaborate on the unusual incidence of impressing a substitute into service. He does identify the man as Simon from Cyrene, a city of Libya in North Africa. Mark additionally identifies him as the father of Alexander and Rufus. Some twenty-five years later, in his letter to the congregation in Rome, Paul takes notes of Rufus and his mother (Romans 16:13). That suggests that Simon, a Passover pilgrim, not only carried the Messiah's cross. He came to believe in the Messiah's mission as well.

The military is in charge of the crucifixion. It occurs at 9 A.M.. Soldiers offer Jesus an opiate. They inscribe the formal charge. They crucify two criminals, one on each side of the central cross. They divide the Messiah's clothing. They throw dice for the robe. They remain at the crucifixion site until Jesus dies. The officer in charge confesses: This man, King of the Jews, is the Son of God! Some like to maintain that this centurion is the first convert. If so, he may represent Gentiles who come into the church as the gospel is proclaimed to all.

Others stand in the shadow of the cross. Priests and scribes regurgitate their accusations. Faithful women watch in bewilderment and grief. Unnamed bystanders misunderstand Jesus' prayer, even though they likely know the words from Psalm 22:1. Unnatural darkness descends at midday. Scripture often employs darkness as symbolic judgment (Isaiah 13:9–11; Joel 2:30–31). Jesus is suffering the punishment and judgment due to the sin of the world. Out of that darkness, at 3 P.M., Jesus testifies to the greatest abandonment of all. He is utterly forsaken. He has been abandoned by the priests of his religion. He has been abandoned by the leaders of his people. He has been abandoned by his closest human companions. He has been abandoned by the motley mob shrieking cries of ignorance. That is bearable. To be abandoned by God is humanly unbearable, even unimaginable. Yet this is precisely what God's Messiah is experiencing. Nonetheless, even out of these depths he cries out to God. He utters a prayer of faith: My God, my God, why? Mark does not record Jesus' final words from his cross. The Messiah declares that his work is finished. He dies with the ancient prayer upon his lips: Father. into your hands I commit my spirit (Luke 23:46; Psalm 31:5).

The sanctuary was the most holy of all holy places in the temple. The High Priest of Israel could enter it but once a year on the solemn Day of Atonement. As death mercifully overtakes Jesus, the inner veil, the curtain separating the Holy of Holies from the Holy Place, is torn from top to bottom. At the hour of the Messiah's death, priests are in the temple, preparing the evening sacrifices, oblivious the greatest truth of humanity's history. The great Day of Atonement is here. The Crucified has offered full atonement for the sins of the world. The struggles of Gethsemane and Golgotha are over, done with once and for all time. Jesus is forsaken and abandoned so that we might never be abandoned. In the life, death and resurrection of his own Son, God is reconciled to us.

The Jewish Sabbath begins at 6 P.M.. After 3 P.M., preparations are being made for a correct observance of its laws and traditions. One member of the Sanhedrin shows remarkable courage. Joseph, who may have related details of the trial to the disciples and the Jerusalem congregation (Acts 1:12–14), secures necessary permission to accord Jesus a descent burial. Criminals were often simply left unburied at the crucifixion mound, which came to be known as place of the skull. As the round stone is rolled against the opening of the tomb it is nearing 6 pm. Israel will rest on the Sabbath and wait for a new day to dawn. Israel's Messiah will rest in the tomb, awaiting the next day when rites of burial will be completed.

Note how Mark involves at least five persons in the burial of Jesus. Joseph of Arimathaea is a respected member of the very council, which adjudged Jesus guilty of blasphemy. Mark carefully adds that he was waiting for the kingdom of God. Pilate is procurator of the Roman province in whose legal jurisdiction the crucifixion was carried out. The centurion is a professional soldier who executed both his duties and his prisoner. The others are Mary Magdalene and Mary the mother of Jesus. They had followed him in Galilee. They had watched the six-hour tragedy. They were part of the final scene of the drama as it came to its ignominious end on the mound known as Golgotha. A wealthy Sadducee, a Gentile politician, a seasoned soldier and two faithful women attest the truth: He was crucified under Pontius Pilate, suffered, died and was buried. The drama of betrayal, abandonment and crucifixion had apparently come to an end.

Discussion:

1. What does the church remember and confess in every celebration of the Eucharist?

2. Creeds help us recall the central acts of Christ's mission and ministry.

3. The early church came to see in Isaiah 52 and 53 descriptions of the Messiah's suffering and death.

Conclusion

Up to this point of his narrative, Mark has traced the heights of the Messiah's popularity and power and the depths of his abandonment and despair. Predictions of the passion are followed by events, which take Jesus step by step to his Via Dolorosa, his way of sorrows. At the end of that path stands the cross, bleak, stark symbol of the termination of a mission and ministry.

One bright moment in the otherwise increasing darkness is the transfiguration on the mount. It affords the disciples a fleeting revelation of the Messiah's glory. The presence of God is assured by the cloud and by the voice, which declares that Jesus' ministry. The kingdom inaugurated by that ministry advanced mightily via preaching, healing, exorcism and miracle. This surrendered to the virtual absence of God. Jesus is bereft of friends, deserted by a wider circle of followers, abandoned by uncomprehending disciples, condemned by spiritually blind religious leaders and rejected by an unprincipled mob. In Gethsemane he struggles to do the Father's will. As he does it, he is all but abandoned by him. The final words of Jesus recorded by Mark in his account of the crucifixion are the Psalmist's prayer of forsakenness.

The church treasures the words spoken by Jesus from Calvary's hill. Drawing from the four Gospels, the church has identified seven "cross words" or last words of Jesus. They have given rise to hymns, liturgies, devotions, holy hours, meditations, sermons and special services of commemoration. Good Friday serves have often featured homilies, which attempt to fathom the depths of meaning in those words. The startling, climatic cry incorporated by Mark in his narrative is known as the fourth word.

That forsakenness is about to give way to grand triumph and victory. The Messiah's ministry is soon to be vindicated. For to each of the passion predictions recorded by Mark is appended the promise of the Messiah's resurrection.

Part Three

Victory and Vindication

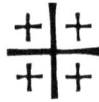

+|+
+|+

CHAPTER TEN

The Messiah is Risen!
Mark 16:1–20

The Crucified One is Not Here! 16:1–8

Mark's narration of the most stupendous event ever recorded in human history seems to be somewhat reserved. The discerning reader might even surmise that it is a bit restrained. The resurrection of Jesus Christ from the dead is, for St. Paul, the source of greatest spiritual certainty and joy. He sketches the awful alternative as he reminds the Christians of Corinth that if Christ is not risen we are still in our sins. That means that our faith is useless and our hope is tragically misplaced. We are of all people most miserable. (1 Corinthians 15:12–20)

So how are we to account for Mark's somber, almost colorless telling of the story? If he is reporting only what he heard from Peter, are we to assume that Peter's telling of the story was equally reserved?

Two reasons may be cited for Mark's apparent restraint. First, Mark is consciously writing to Christians (but so was Paul!). His readers confess and believe in the risen and living Lord. Mark does not have to prove the reality of the resurrection. Neither does he have to provide anecdotal details of the great event. Jesus was a living presence in their assembly as they worshipped, remembered, celebrated and prayed (Acts 2:42.). His readers are fully aware that the resurrection of their Lord is the foundation of their faith and hope. Secondly, if Mark is writing specifically for the congregation in the city of Rome, he is addressing a troubled church. It is, in fact, facing the very trials and tribulations foretold by Jesus. The abrupt ending of his record speaks of the amazement and fears felt by the disciples even when they were told the incredible news: He is risen! Christians in Rome face astonishment and fears as the Neronian persecutions fall upon them. Mark's subdued and somber tone may reflect the experiences of messianic community.

After Sabbath rest, at daybreak the third day (Sunday), women discover-
er that they need not worry about the stone. The sealed tomb is open.
A young man, elsewhere identified as an angel (messenger), heralds the
startling news. You are seeking Jesus, the Nazarene who was crucified.
He has arisen as he promised (8:31; 9:31; 10:33–34). Tell the disciples
that he goes before them in to Galilee (14:28). That is the world, the
joyous gospel of assurance and restoration so desperately needed by
the disciples. In spite of their denial of him, he will not deny them.
In spite of their cowardice, he will not forsake them. In spite of their
abandonment of him, he will not abandon them. And those faithful
women who came to the tomb are to be sure to tell Peter the good
news. In spite of his boasting, bravado and broken promises, the Savior
will not abandon him!

At this juncture of his narrative, Mark reminds us that the risen Messiah had not yet revealed himself. The disciples have not as yet seen the
risen Lord. He has not as yet met them in Galilee. The disciples and
women are amazed. They are afraid.

The Longer Ending of Mark: Proclaim the Gospel 16:9–20

Mark is unique among the Four Gospels in that it poses the apparently
puzzling problem of multiple endings. Reliable early manuscripts,
which we currently possess, agree that Mark concludes his work at
what, for the sake of convenience, translators call v.8. Among these
Greek are two, which are known among scholars as Codex Sinaiticus
(Aleph) and Codex Vaticanus (B). Both date from the fourth century.
Both omit vss. 9–20 as do a number of early translations or versions in
other languages. The longer ending, known as the Canonical Ending,
comprises 16:9–20. This is found in two fifth century Greek manuscripts known as Codex Alexandrinus (A) and Codex Bezae (D). It is
also part of the Markan text in later Greek manuscripts. Some suggest
that I might actually be a fragment of an early Easter sermon, which
some copyist inserted in the text. It is found in many early and later
versions without any indication that it is not considered to be an integral part of the book. Another alternative ending is named the Shorter
Ending. It is but one verse and follows 16:8. It states that Jesus sent
out the sacred message of salvation from east to west through the ministry of Peter and his companions. Still another alternate reading is

the so-called Freer Logion, named after the manuscript in which it is found. It often appears between vss. 14 and 15. It declares that the age of unbelief, which lies under the rule of Satan, has expired. Jesus was delivered into death so that sinners might inherit the glory of heaven.

Careful readers readily recognize that 16:8 does represent an abrupt conclusion to this Gospel. It is widely held that an original ending, composed by Mark, was somehow separated from the original text, which is not longer extant. Or it may have been excised from copies made from Mark's text to be circulated among the churches. Others are still convinced that Mark deliberately and somewhat dramatically intended to conclude his account at 16:8 for reasons cited above. If that is the case, alternate endings were composed at a later date to compensate for its supposedly original abruptness. This is not the place to discuss the merits of various views.

An acceptable explanation of the Canonical Ending is to see in it an attempt to reflect the consciousness of the early church of its great mandate to proclaim the gospel and baptize in the Messiah's name. Special gifts accorded the disciples were gradually exercised less and less in and by the early church. One thing remains constant: Proclaim the good news of the kingdom, which has come in the life, death and resurrection of God's Messiah. This is supported by the explicit commission, which is recorded at the close of the Gospel of Matthew. The church does not base its teachings or its practices upon uncertain, unclear or disputed passages of Holy Scripture. Yet it can look upon 16:9–20 as confirming its continuing witness to Jesus, Son of God, Messiah and gloriously living Lord.

Conclusion

Power and popularity, suffering and abandonment, victory and vindication – these may be viewed as three acts of the dramatic narrative, which witnesses that Jesus of Nazareth is God's Messiah. The grand climax of the drama, Act III, as it were, is resurrection. It is not only the reversal of suffering and abandonment. It is God's powerful vindication of the challenging claims made by and about Jesus.

In the opening sentence of his Gospel, Mark declares that Jesus is both Messiah and Son of God. This initial declaration is repeated in the narrative three times. Twice it is asserted by a voice from out of heaven. Once it stems form a totally unlikely source. It is voiced by the Roman officer who stands at the crucifixion scene. Each testifies to the unassailable truth, which is witnessed by Mark. Jesus is in all truth Messiah and Son of God. He fulfilled his promises to rise from suffering and death to life.

An intriguing and fascinating facet of Mark's Gospel, assuming that 16:8 is its original ending, is the absence of data relating a reunion of the risen Lord with the apostles. Women are commissioned by the messenger in the empty tomb to tell the disciples that they will see Jesus in Galilee. Mark drops the matter at that point. Why doesn't he at least comment on it? It must have been a truly unforgettable meeting between the risen Savior and those who had so painfully forsaken him. Some have not too fortuitously dubbed this "the Markan secret." Whatever one chooses to call it, the fact remains that Mark does not record what happened later Easter Sunday morning (John) or Sunday afternoon (Luke), that evening (John) or the following Sunday evening (John).

A number of speculative suggestions have been offered. 1) Mark simply is not concerned about it. That seems unlikely. If Mark is the interpreter of Peter, he had probably heard about that meeting and the impression it made on the disciples a hundred times. Commentators surmise that Mark and others must have listed with rapt attention as an again peter told and retold the story. One could hardly simply ignore its importance. 2) Mark attempts to play down prominence given the apostles in order not to arouse undue attention from the authorities. This is also unlikely. Nero and his magistrates would have files on them and their activities. 3) Mark intentionally omits anything that would put the spotlight on the apostles. The congregation in Rome, capital city of the empire, was not founded by an apostle. That might be a sensitive issue with some. But that, too, is highly unlikely. At the end of the century Clement of Rome writes a letter to the church in Corinth. In it he admonishes his fellow believers to show proper respect for their presbyters (elders: pastors). Clement shows neither hesitancy nor sensitivity in regard to apostolic founding. That concern emerged at a later time. 4) Mark is restrained by his noble concern and high esteem for St. Paul. Paul was not one of the original twelve. Too much emphasis upon a reunion of Jesus with the eleven might tend to put Paul in an unfavorable light.

Resources

Selected readings from Luther"s Large Catechism (1529). Citations are by page and paragraph of Theodore G. Tappert's translation of the *Book of Concord* (Muhenberg Press, 1959). They are intended to encourage exploration of Luther's powerful witness to what he identifies as the heritage of Christendom from ancient times.

Chapter 1

1. We can know nothing of Christ unless it is offered by the preaching of the gospel (415,38).

2. Through his word, God gives the Holy Spirit to offer the treasure of salvation (415,38).

3. The entire gospel depends on the proper understanding of the birth, passion, resurrection and ascension of Christ (415,33).

Chapter 2

1. There was no help until the Son of God had mercy on our misery and came to help (414,29).

2. Satan and all powers are subject to Christ (414,31).

3. Satan seeks to tear us from faith, hope and love. He wants to drive us to despair (434,104).

Chapter 3

1. In the church we have forgiveness through the holy sacraments and absolution (417,54).

2. Confession consists of two parts: I lament my sin. God absolves me (458,15).

3. Absolution is a great treasure to be accepted with praise and gratitude (459,22).

Chapter 4

1. I yearn for God's word, absolution and the sacraments (461,33).

2. Baptism brings victory over death (441,41).

3. The Holy Spirit will completely sanctify us. We wait for this in faith (419,62).

Chapter 5

1. The flesh does not trust God. We sin daily in word and deed (432,89).
2. We sin with eyes and ears, hands, body and soul (413,22).
3. To be baptized is to be baptized by God himself (438,14).

Chapter 6

1. To have a god is to trust in something with one's whole heart (365,2).
2. Money and possessions are the most common idol on earth (367,57).
3. Where God's word is preached and believed, the cross will not be far away (429,65).

Chapter 7

1. One who knows the Ten Commandments perfectly knows the entire Scriptures (361,17).
2. Commandments do not of themselves make us Christians. The Creed brings grace (419,67).
3. To fear, love and trust in the one true God is to fulfill all commandments (409,324).

Chapter 8

1. God's kingdom comes through word and faith (427,53).
2. The Holy Spirit works through his word to grant forgiveness (418,58).
3. The Holy Spirit makes me holy. He illuminates hearts to cling to the word (416,40).

Chapter 9

1. The Sacrament of the Altar is the true body and blood of the Lord Christ in and under bread and wine. It is comprehended in God's word and connected with it (447,8).
2. Everyone who wishes to be a Christian and go to the sacrament should be familiar with it. We do not admit to the sacrament

those who do not know what they seek (447,2).

3. We go to the sacrament because we receive there forgiveness of sins. Why? Because the words are through which it is imparted (449,22).

Chapter 10

1. The Redeemer has brought us from death to life, from sin to righteousness. He became man that he might become Lord over sin and death. He devoured death and ascended into heaven and assumed dominion at the right hand of the Father (414,31).

2. The Holy Spirit sees to it that sin does not harm us because we are in the Christian church. He orders everything though word and sacraments (418,55).

3. What is the kingdom of God? God sent our Lord into the world to redeem and deliver us and bring us to himself. To this end he gives the Holy Spirit to enlighten and strengthen us in faith and by his power (426,51).

Witness to Ministry

According to the Gospel of Luke

Introduction

Toward the end of the second century, the renowned Church Father, Origen of Alexandria, judged that while heretical sectarians boast of many gospels, the church recognized but Four Gospels. He writes that the Third is that KATA LOUKAN, what we customarily call The Gospel According to Luke. Some thirty years earlier the Muratorian Canon had attributed the Third Gospel to Luke, physician and companion of Paul, who composed in his own name the book that came to bear his name. At about the same time Irenaeus, a prolific writer and stalwart defender of the Christian Faith against assorted heresies, identified Luke as the disciple of Paul who recorded the gospel preached by the apostle.

Two centuries later the Latin Father, Jerome, declared that Luke, physician and native of Antioch in Syria, penned the Gospel, which was highly prized by Paul. Jerome, a linguist who gave the church the Vulgatta, the Latin translation of the Bible, comments that Luke was not only learned in medicine, but in Greek language as well. The language of both Luke and Acts is, to be sure, exceptionally eloquent. This has been noted by countless scholars who probe the internal and external evidence to determine the origin and authorship of the work we know as The Gospel of Luke.

The man whom tradition early credited with the authorship of this Gospel (and The Acts of the Apostles) is mentioned three times in the New Testament. Luke is a fellow-worker and devoted companion of Paul (Philemon 24; 2 Timothy 4:11). The third reference (Colossians 4:10–14) clearly identifies him as the beloved Gentile physician. The New Testament is sadly silent regarding the circumstances under which Paul and Luke became associates. Tarsus, the home of Paul, boasted a famous medical school. It has been surmised that their friendship was established when Luke was a student in Tarsus and long before Paul became a Christian. As genial as this speculation is, one must say that it was not common for a Pharisee, even a Pharisee who was a Roman citizen, to forge a strong friendship with a Gentile, unless Luke had become a Hebrew proselyte. Significant passages from Acts suggest that Luke spent considerable time with Paul during his missionary ministry. This undoubtedly led the early church to conclude that Luke was not only an able disciple of Paul, but also a powerful Greek witness to Paul's preaching. Some even conjecture that Luke was to Paul what Mark was to Peter. Some believe that Luke is the unnamed brother whom Paul singularly honored for his ministry in the gospel, the good news of God's saving action in Jesus Christ. If Luke is the author of Luke through Acts, it means that a Gentile has authored more of the New Testament than any other individual writer.

Regardless of its authorship, students of this Gospel are fairly unanimous in claiming that it was written for Gentile readers. The author (we shall name him Luke) intended in the first instance to provide an orderly and accurate account to inform a certain Theophilos of the true ministry of Jesus (1:1–4). Theophilos is accorded the title, "most excellent." This common term was widely used among high-ranking officials in the Roman government. It is quite possible, perhaps even likely, that he had been instructed in the Christian Faith and desired more instruction and reliable evidence before he committed himself to Christ.

Luke, in contrast to Matthew, shows little concern for linking the ministry of Jesus to Old Testament prophecy. Citations from the Old Testament are, in fact, rare. When they appear they are drawn from the Septuagint (LXX), the standard Greek Version. Luke traces the descent of Jesus not to Abraham, father of the covenant people, but to Adam, the father of all nations. His vocabulary reflects his intent to communicate with Greek readers. He regularly substitutes Greek words for Hebrew, Latin and Aramaic expressions. Colloquialisms are restored to Greek for. He employs precise Greek medical terms. He uses Roman time and recognizes Roman or imperial rule. His preface (1:1–4) is an example of superb classical Greek. It is sometimes labeled the best Greek found in the entire New Testament, including the letters of Paul.

In addition to being physician and evangelist, Luke was an eminent historian. He engaged in thorough research before composing his work. He sets his narrative of the ministry of the ministry of Jesus within a carefully delineated historical context. The ministry of John, herald and forerunner of Jesus, is precisely tied to the reign of Tiberius and to the rule of tetrarchs and high priests (3:1–2). The birth narrative is firmly linked to Caesar Augustus, an imperial census, a provincial governor and a specific city whose historical significance is accurately sketched. A parallel is found in the Roman historian Tacitus. In his Annales he refers to Christus, from whom the sect of Christians is named. He was executed at the hands of the procurator Pontius Pilate in the reign of Tiberius.

Caesar Augsutus (63 B.C. - A.D. 14) was the grandnephew, adopted son and heir of Julius Caesar. He actually bore the name, Gaius Octavius (or Octavian). Upon death of Julius Caesar in 44 B.C., he assumed the name Gaius Julius Caesar. In 27 B.C. the Roman Senate conferred on the title, Augustus (majestic or sublime). Tiberius, adopted son of Augustus, became emperor in A.D. 14. Herod I, known as Herod the Great (74–4 B.C.), was made king of Palestine in 37 B.C.. His son, Archelaus, became ethnarch (literally: ruler of people) of Judea, Samaria and Idumea. He was deposed A.D. 6 and replaced by a Roman governor. Pontius Pilate was the fifth governor (A.D. 26–36). Herod Antipas, brother of Archelaus, was tetrarch (literally: a fourth part) of Galilee and Perea (4 B.C. – A.D. 39). After years of corrupt and dissolute rule, he was banished to Gaul. Herod Philip (4 B.C. – A.D. 33) rebuilt the city of Paneas and dedicated it to the emperor. It was known thereafter as Caesarea Philippi. Luke's careful identification firmly anchors the beginnings and development of Christianity within imperial and national history.

Luke demonstrates a historian's sense of the importance of persons. He alone makes reference to Naaman the Syrian (4:23), Zacharias the priest (1:5), Theudas the revolutionary (Acts 5:26) and Herod Agrippa the king (Acts 12:1ff). Luke accords high treatment to women. In both Gentile and Jewish societal structure, women were routinely relegated to decidedly inferior status. A Jewish male daily thanked God that the Creator had not made him a Gentile, a slave or a female. Luke praises Elizabeth and Mary (1:5–56), mothers of John and Jesus. He includes in his narrative the ministry of Anna who recognized in the Child of Bethlehem what many in Israel failed to perceive (2:38). A woman showed more courtesy to our Lord than did his host (7:36–50).

Mary Magdalene, Joanna and Susanna are described as ministering to the Lord out of their own resources (8:1–3). Mary and Martha serve as contrasting examples of discipleship (10:38–42). Luke portrays in vivid detail the ministry of women who came to render final service to their Lord, only to find an empty tomb and hear the astounding news: He is not here. His is risen! (23:55–24:11).

The third Gospel evinces remarkable concern for the role of the Holy Spirit. Reference to God's Spirit is made fifty-three times in Luke through Acts. The first two chapters of the Lukan Prologue are almost a commentary on the work of the Spirit in preparing for the ministry of Christ. Zachariah is informed that his son, John, will be filled with the Holy Spirit. Mary is assured that the Spirit is with her. Elizabeth is filled with the Holy Spirit as she sings her song of praise. Zachariah is filled with the Holy Spirit as he intones the Benedictus. John the Baptizer is strengthened by the Spirit as he inaugurates the messianic era. The Spirit prompts aged Simon to recognize in the Holy Child the Messiah of God. Jesus himself is guided by the Spirit, via baptism and wilderness testing, into his ministry (3:21–22; 4:1–14) to seek and save the lost (19:9–10).

The third Gospel is rich in instances of prayer and praise. Luke alone records the four great hymns sung by the church: the Magnificat (1:46–55); the Benedictus (1:68–79); the Gloria in Excelsis (2:14); and the Nunc Dimittus (2:29–32). Luke alone is sensitive to the fact that Jesus prays at crisis moments of his life and ministry; prior to his baptism (3:21); before his initial conflict with the teachers of the law (5:16); before he chooses the Twelve (6:12); prior to the first prediction of his passion (9:18); at his transfiguration (9:29); before he teaches his disciples to pray (11:1); and while hanging on the cross (23:46). Prayers and praise are frequently linked. It was been noted by more than one serious reader that the third Gospel begins and ends in the Temple, where people are praising God (1:9; 24:53).

Luke lays particular stress upon the scope of salvation accomplished by the ministry of Jesus. Matthew, Mark and John record the words of Isaiah 40:3 as predictive of the role of John the Baptizer in preparing the way for Jesus. Luke alone adds the citation, which asserts the universal character of Jesus' ministry: "All flesh shall see the salvation of God" (3:4–6). Luke is ever aware that the good news of great joy

heralded by the angel over Bethlehem's fields is truly for all. Samaritans, despised by Jews, are not excluded from the kingdom of God because they are Samaritans. Luke recounts the healing of ten lepers, of
which only he gave thanks: a Samaritan (17:11–19). Gentiles are not
peremptorily excluded on the basis of race. Luke recounts that Jesus
found the quality of faith in a Roman centurion, which he never found
in Israel (7:1–10). Indeed, the good news includes the then revolutionary notion that the Christ who was set to be a light for revelation
to the Gentiles (2:32) assures us that many will come from all people
to sit at the table and share in the messianic feast of salvation (13:29).
Luke wants to make sure that Theophilus understand this universal
scope of the saving work of Christ.

Luke's narration has been characterized as sketching the most comprehensive portrait of Jesus' ministry. No Gospel qualifies for what in
modern literature is known as personal biography. None purports to
trace intimate details of his life. Outside of the final week of his earthly
life, there are huge gaps in the story. The years between his presentation
in the Temple (2:21–24) and his appearance for Passover at the age of
twelve (2:41–52) have been filled with fanciful and often bizarre tales.
Of the years intervening before he began his public ministry at the
age of thirty (3:21–22) we have absolutely no reliable evidence. Luke
does not cover events of his life from the prologue to his ministry to
the earthly completion of that ministry at his ascension. Additionally,
Luke records more miracles, parables and incidents unique to his Gospel than any other Evangelist.

The theme of the third Gospel is found in Jesus' own pronouncement
to Zacchaeus: "The Son of Man came to seek and save that which was
lost" (19:9–10). This is his mission and ministry. Luke's witness to that
ministry served to instruct Theophilus. It serves today to confront us
with the saving acts of God revealed in the life, death, resurrection
and glorification of his Son, the Savior who is Christ the Lord (2:11).
It leads us into the profound truth that Christ should suffer and rise
from the dead so that repentance and forgiveness of sins might be proclaimed in his name to all nations (24:46ff). Iranaeus writes that after
the resurrection, the Gospel writers were filled with the power of the
Holy Spirit. They had perfect knowledge and went to the ends of the
earth proclaiming the good news and announcing heavenly peace to

mankind. That may be a bit of an overstatement, but it reveals the high regard the early church had for the Gospels.

In that spirit, the church receives and acknowledges the canon of Sacred Scripture as the written word of God. Inspiration, as the brief historical introduction to Luke clearly demonstrates (1:1–4), does not preclude careful research and use of materials on the part of biblical writers. Neither does it somehow annul their humanness and turn living penmen into lifeless, robot-like pens. It does assure that we have in the Gospel According to Luke an authoritative witness to the saving ministry to Jesus Christ. As we study this witness, we ask the Holy Spirit to instill trust in Christ, through whom we have the knowledge of salvation and forgiveness of sins through the mercy of our God (1:67ff).

For use within Lutheran congregations or by other interested persons or groups, selected readings from Martin Luther's Large Catechism of 1529 are listed for each chapter in the Resources. Citations are by page and paragraph of Theodore G. Tappert's translation of the *Book of Concord* (Muhenberg Press, 1959). They are intended to encourage exploration of Luther's powerful witness to what he identifies as the heritage of Christendom from ancient times.

Part One

Prologue and Preparation

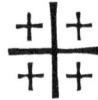

╬

CHAPTER ONE

Prologue to Ministry
Luke 1:1–4:13

Great news for all people: A Savior is born who is Christ our Lord.

God Acts in Human History 1:5–80

The most astounding events in all human history have unfolded as the drama of divine intervention and human response. Many have recorded and retold the story. The Gospel of Mark, composed circa 65, is very likely one of these accounts handed down from eyewitnesses. Luke wants to be certain that his witness to the ministry of Jesus is orderly, accurate and totally reliable.

Main Characters of the Drama

Zachariah was a Levitical priest, one of some 20,000 who, each year, served at least two one-week courses according to lot. All priests served in the Temple only at the great Old Testament Feasts of Passover, Pentecost and Tabernacles (Leviticus 23). His wife Elizabeth was also of Aaronic descent. They were childless, which was a mark of God's displeasure for a Jewish couple of that day. The couple saw in the angelic announcement a two-fold blessing. A son will remove the stigma of shame. That son, filled with the Holy Spirit, will prepare the way of the Lord. In Hebrew tradition the prophet Elijah would somehow return to inaugurate the messianic age.

Mary of Nazareth, in Galilee, had been betrothed to a certain Joseph who could claim lineage from the royal house of David. Betrothal was tantamount to marriage. Gabriel greets her as one highly graced or favored. Her son will be named Jesus, meaning Savior. Known as the Son of God, he will be given a kingdom, which, unlike the monarchy of Israel, will endure forever. In deep faith, Mary acknowledges her chosen role. Prompted by the Holy Spirit, Elizabeth cries out that Mary is blessed among all women.

The Magnificat

This grand and noble hymn of Mary derives its name, as do all the Lukan hymns, from its beginning Latin words. Drawing heavily on Hannah's paean of praise recorded in 1 Samuel 2:1–10, the hymn is a truly magnificent confession of Mary's faith in God, her Savior. She puts her complete trust in the word God had spoken to her. Her deep faith and humility are an example for the people of God of every generation, which recognizes her blessedness.

The Benedictus

This stately hymn, incorporated in the liturgy of the church, is the spirit-filled response of Zachariah to God's gracious action. God has remembered his promise to deliver his people by providing salvation, forgiveness and peace. All who sit in spiritual darkness may experience the light of God's gracious redemption. Zachariah not only has a son; his son is the prophet who is to prepare the way for God's coming to his people.

The Birth of Jesus 2:1–52

Judea belonged to the Roman province of Syria. A census occurred every fourteen years in order to levy taxes and compile lists for compulsory military training. One of the distinct privileges Jews enjoyed under Roman rule was exemption from the military. This census was primarily for taxation. It was held sometime between our calendar reckoning of 8–4 B.C.

Journey to Bethlehem 2:1–20

Bethlehem was a small village with a few accommodations for travelers. Mary laid her first-born son in the place animals were tethered by the lodge. Shepherds were among the simplest and most uneducated persons in Judea. Religious rigorists tended to despise them because they could not observe the fine points of the Mosaic Law. These particular shepherds may have been keepers of the flocks from which Temple offerings were taken. If so, the symbolism is compelling; those who cared for the lambs of God tend The Lamb of God! In similar vein, the angelic choir may have substituted for the band of musicians who customarily greeted a newborn son. At any rate, the hymn of angels, know as the Gloria in Excelsis Deo, praises God for the gift of Christ the Lord. Shepherds, angles and Mary are examples of response to the advent of the Son of God. They seek him out; they rejoice in his coming; they ponder the meaning of the magnificent message of the birth.

Recognition in the Temple 2:21–40

Circumcision, Presentation and Purification are meticulously kept in accord with Mosaic prescription (Genesis 17:9–14); Exodus 13:2; Leviticus 12: Numbers 18:16). Jesus fulfills the law of God as part of his redemptive ministry. Simeon is moved by the Holy Spirit to intone the fourth great Lukan hymn, the Nunc Dimittus. Jesus, the light of the world, is the true glory of Israel who brings saving revelation to Gentiles. But his ministry engenders opposition. He proclaims the need for repentance over sin, forgiveness of sin and a turning from sin to the new life of obedience. This does not sit well with human pride, self-sufficiency and egocentric determination.

Anna had known great sorrow in her long life. Yet she served God in the Temple. Sharing Simeon's faith, she witnessed to all awaiting redemption of Jerusalem. Luke passes over the years between these events and the return of Jesus to the Temple with a physician's viewpoint: The child grew and developed physically, mentally and spiritually.

A Son Comes Home 2:41–52

All adult males were expected to attend the Passover in Jerusalem if at all possible. A Jewish boy attained spiritual maturity at the age of twelve, becoming a "son of the law." Distraught parents finally discover their missing son in the precincts of the Temple, hearing and questioning a group of rabbis. There is mild rebuke on the part of both parents and son. Jesus firmly exclaims that the incident is not a chance happening. He must be in the house of his real Father. But he understands the difficulty Mary and Joseph have in grasping that. He returns to Nazareth and lives the life of an obedient son. Luke, again with keen insight, remarks that Jesus continues to develop intellectually, physically, spiritually and socially. The Son of God knows what being human entails.

Baptism and Testing 3:1–3:13

The carefully crafted six-fold political and religious dating provides a reliably fixed historical point for the preparatory ministry of John the Baptizer. Caiaphas was actually High Priest. Annas had served earlier and continued to be a powerful voice in religious affairs.

Voice in the Wilderness 3:1–20

Luke understands the activity of John in terms of the prophetic utterance of Isaiah. John emerges as a radical preacher of repentance. He thundered the law of God, which always judges and condemns. He castigated his own people for the self-justifying notion that physical descent from Abraham automatically assured them of exemption from judgment of God over sin. But he proclaimed the gospel as he pointed to the Anointed One who would pour out the Spirit upon them. The tetrarch deserved special rebuke for his offensive lifestyle. He had seduced Herodias, his own niece and wife of his half-brother and brazenly installed her as his queen. Partly in anger and because he feared John's influence over the people, Herod imprisoned John and finally decreed his death.

God's Beloved Son 3:21–38

At the age of thirty, Jesus begins his so-called public ministry. The New Testament is uniformly silent regarding the intervening years of the Lord's life. At his baptism, Jesus reinforces his identity with humankind, as does Luke's genealogy. The son of Adam is baptized by word and symbol to be God's own beloved Son. The words recorded by Luke are taken from Psalm 2:7, a description of the messianic King and from Isaiah 42:1, describing the suffering servant of God. Already at his baptism, the cross of Jesus casts its shadow over him, the Servant who came to seek and save the perishing.

Tried and Tested 4:1–13

The Holy Spirit, symbolized by a dove, almost immediately leads Jesus into the wilderness, which stretched between the Judean plateau and the Dead Sea. It was known as the place of devastation. His ministry is subjected to severe testing from a totally different spirit: the devil (Greek: diabolos). Forty days conjures up the image of Israel's forty years of wandering in the wilderness in pursuit of the land of promise.

Luke cites three crucial temptations (testings). Each is basic to human existence and values. We require more than bread for the body, as vital as that it. We need the life sustaining word of God. We need more than a sense of power over life and the lives of others. We must acknowledge the God whose creatures we ever remain. We require more than momentary and instant gratification. We must commit our life to God whose promises never fail. In each instance Jesus quotes Scripture (Deuteronomy 8:3; 6:13; 10:20; 6:16; Psalm 91:11–12) Jesus views his ministry in terms of seeing and saving humankind, not in attaining immediate power or glory for himself by any means available.

Summary

The good news of great joy has been announced. In the birth of Jesus, the Savior of the world has come. God carefully prepared for the unique historical event. The Holy Spirit attends in a most remarkable manner people who set the stage for the ministry of Christ the Lord. At the appropriate time the Holy Spirit prepares the Father's only-begotten Son for his role in the drama of salvation. A tried and tested Jesus is ready to embark upon his ministry in the abiding power of the Spirit. But the way will not be smooth. Luke observes that Satan, having finished all his testings, left Jesus for a period of time. Post-baptismal testings were neither the first nor last attempts to divert our Lord from his divinely ordained work.

Discussion:

1. Does unknown authorship of the third Gospel make it any less authoritative for the church?

2. Does tradition help or hinder the contemporary church in distinguishing fact from pious speculation?

3. Which characteristics of the four hymns in Luke ought to be found in modern hymnody and liturgy?

4. What does it mean to be filled with the Holy Spirit?

5. Why are the testings of Jesus crucial to understanding his ministry? Is there occurrence immediately after his baptism and just prior to his public ministry particularly significant?

CHAPTER TWO

Ministry and Preparation
Luke 4:14–6:49

The Son of Man is Lord of the Sabbath

In the Power of the Spirit 4:14–5:26

The Holy Spirit now leads Jesus into the northern area of Palestine known as Galilee (literally: a circle). It was described as the highlands. Its benign climate and adequate water supply assured its enviable fertility. In Jesus' day, Galilee, with neighboring Perea, was the political domain of Herod Antipas (4 B.C. – A.D. 39). Galilee was also a hot bed of insurrection. This helps explain why the tetrarch was fearful of John's activities. Roman power had little patience with seditionists or puppet princes who failed to control them.

In the Synagogue 4:14–30

The Temple in Jerusalem was the appointed sanctuary for sacrificial and religious cultus. It was under the rigid control of the Levitical priesthood headed up by the High Priest and the wealthy, aristocratic sect of Sadducees. Synagogues were local centers of worship and teaching. They were the domain of elders and scribes, experts in the interpretation of Jewish law. They generally belonged to the sect of Pharisees, whose very name denotes separated ones. Taking the Commandments (Exodus 20; Deuteronomy 5) as their basic text, they added, refined, elaborated and reinterpreted rules, regulations and rabbinic lore. This came to be known as the oral law or traditions. Pharisees were of their religious code. Unfortunately, these legalists sought salvation, not in the grace of God, but in scrupulous observance of their traditions. They utterly failed to see the spiritual reality that lay beyond rite, ritual and rule.

Synagogue worship consisted of creed (Deuteronomy 6:4–5), reading of Scripture in ancient Hebrew and modern Aramaic, prayer and blessing. Exposition or discussion of reading was led by a qualified worshipper invited to do so by the local Chazzam or director. Jesus read from the scroll of Isaiah 61 and interpreted it in terms of his own calling. The congregation became incensed because of his favorable reference to Gentiles and because of his claim to fulfillment.

Ministry of Miracles 4:31–5:15

In the power of the Spirit, Jesus launches his ministry of healing. Jewish exorcists possessed a wide – and sometimes bizarre – range of formulae and ritual. Jesus steers clear of it all by simply uttering an imperious word. His authority and power are awesome even though so unpretentiously exercised. Peter's mother-in-law, in the grip of a major fever (so Luke the physician), experiences healing; this moves the multitudes to seek healing for various illnesses. Demons shout out: You are the Son of God! At this early state of his ministry Jesus thwarts any rash enthusiasm that could easily spark rebellion and result in disaster.

Our Lord's ministry early focuses on people who will play permanent roles in his mission. Peter, James and John constitute a sort of inner circle. Lake Gannesaret, known as well as the Sea of Galilee or Tiberius, was some thirteen miles long by eight miles wide. The miracle of the nets fills seasoned fishermen with the realization of dependence on his grace. Sinful people need a sin-bearing Savior. Jesus' ministry of word and deed is carried on in synagogue and house, village and barren desert are, in boat and at the seashore. The good news of the Savior who is Christ the Lord must be proclaimed.

Our Lord's ministry of healing is not to be denied the most distressed of all. Leprosy was so dreaded an illness that specific hygienic laws went into effect as soon as it was detected (Leviticus 13:34ff). Leprosy brought physical, social and psychological isolation from family and community. This particular man had a severe (so Luke the physician) case. Jesus grants him the healing touch. Yet he does not exempt him from fulfilling prescribed rituals. The miraculous ministry of Jesus is never pitted against normal spiritual or medical processes.

Law and Forgiveness 5:16–26

Teachers of the law, as well as Pharisees, begin to take note of Jesus' ministry. Luke recounts a specific incident, which triggers the opposition, which continues to widen the gulf between a basically law and grace approach to religion. Jews viewed suffering in the context of sin(s). Without voicing any judgment as to the correctness of fallacy of this assumption, Jesus deals with the need at hand. He absolves the man of his sins. Scribes and Pharisees present see this bold act as a blatant case of blasphemy. Only God can forgive sins. They reason quite correctly that Jesus is claiming for himself a unique divine prerogative. Aware of their thinking – and to effect what to their minds was the logical consequence of forgiveness – Jesus heals the paralytic. Luke records the utter astonishment, which gripped them all. We can only hope that Jesus' detractors were also moved to glorify God in response to the amazing things they had seen.

The Kingdom of God 5:27–6:49

The early church identified Levi with the Apostle Matthew (Matthew 9:9–13). He is called a Teloones, a collector of taxes. Luke includes in his full and reliable account a parable in which a tax collector play a prominent, instructive role (18:9–14). The Roman Empire had an elaborate and efficient system of taxation. However, district assessment could easily open the door to exploitation and corruption. Collectors were usually able to pocket huge sums of revenue. Taxes and duties were so burdensome that the common people linked collectors with thieves, murderers and prostitutes. They were grouped together as notorious sinners and societal parasites. In spite of this, Jesus chooses Levi as he speaks the simple word: Follow me! Jesus' willingness to dine with outcasts not unexpectedly causes self-righteous judges considerable consternation. Jesus' reply is as direct as it is out of harmony with their notions of spirituality. Dr. Luke undoubtedly found immense pleasure in recording it.

The Company of Christ 5:27–39

To this point in Luke's narration, Jesus has summoned Peter, James, John and Levi (Matthew) to discipleship. There is an old adage: If you can't attack the king, start with the ministers. The disciples of Jesus do not follow the rigid fasting (Monday and Thursday) and ritualistic prayer (noon, 3 P.M.,

6 P.M.) requirements imposed by the teachers of the law. To Jesus'
mind, discipleship may be likened to a wedding celebration filled with
joy. The days will come when Jesus will be taken from his disciples.
Then they can fast in sorrow. Furthermore, the disciples of Jesus are
not to be bound to the old ways of doing and thinking religion. Jesus did not come to put Band-Aid patches on a worn out system. His
ministry is to call sinners to repentance. Genuine repentance includes
grasping the grace of God, which bestows forgiveness and spiritual re-
newal. This must take the place of old self-striving, self-satisfying and
self-justifying efforts of misguided legalists in their quest to earn divine favor and salvation.

Opposition to the Kingdom 6:1–11

Ever since the cure of the paralytic (5:18–26) the opponents of Jesus
were seeking to find charges they might level against him. They find a
critical accusation in a serious supposed violation of the Sabbath. Eating from a cornfield was neither a legal crime nor an immoral act (Deuteronomy 23:25). The charge is that the disciples do so on a holy day.
Some of the Pharisees witnessing the incident (what are they doing
there on the Sabbath?) are quick to label them Sabbath breakers. Jesus
refuses to be led into a lengthy, arid discourse regarding the technical
minutiae governing Sabbath behavior. He cites an incident involving
David (1 Samuel 21:1–6). David and his comrades in arms eat of the
twelve loaves dedicated each Sabbath to the glory of God's presence
with Israel. Only priests were to eat the loaves (Leviticus 24:5–9). David puts human need above religious ritual. Jesus imposes one supreme
law: The Son of Man is Lord of the Sabbath.

To reap, thrash and winnow on the Sabbath was, to a Pharisee, a grave
infraction of the law. To heal on the Sabbath – and in the very synagogue where the law was rehearsed – was an unspeakably heinous act.
The man's right hand (so Luke the physician) was useless. Apocryphal
tradition surmises that the man was a stone mason whose deformity
rendered him unfit for work. To treat a person in a life threatening
circumstance was permissible on the Sabbath. This man obviously did
not fall into that category. The Lord of the Sabbath simply invokes
the higher law of mercy over regulation. The legal experts, in the synagogue to spy on Jesus, react with insane anger. Our Lord may well have

lodged a counter charge. God's people attend God's house to worship. Hypocrites are there to find fault, detect the slightest hint of unorthodox practice and condemn those who fail to measure up to their self-devised standards of piety.

Jesus Calls His Apostles 6:12–19

After a night of solitary prayer and fellowship with his Father in heaven, Jesus formally selects those who constitute his closest fellowship on earth. From his disciples, those who had been following him, Jesus calls the twelve whom he names apostles (literally: sent-out ones). Our Lord uses all manner of persons for service in his kingdom. Simon belonged to the sect of Zealots, fanatical revolutionaries who sought to free Israel from any foreign domination. The apostles accompany him to the plain where Jesus preaches, heals and exorcises demons.

Foundation for Living 6:20–49

The Sermon on the Plain, titled also the Sermon on the Mount, begins with a series of logia (sayings) known as Beatitudes (Latin: Beati, blessed or happy). They have been called verbal bombshells because they shatter goals and values pretty much prized by the world.

Inverted Standards 6:20–38

It is absolutely vital to recall that Jesus speaks these passages to his disciples. They relate to life in his kingdom, life in relationship to the Son of Man. They are not a political code. Furthermore, Jesus lays great stress on hearing. It is one thing to listen, another to hear and understand what is being spoken. The often-called golden rule of love in action is, strictly speaking, not original with Jesus. But Jesus casts it in a positive form. Key to this inversion of standards is the word, love (Greek: agape). This is not erotic, passionate, sentimental or even affectionate love; it is benevolent, caring clove, which seeks only to bestow well-being on another. Such love is not deserved; but it is rewarded by a merciful and loving God who is ever gracious in his dealings with us. Jesus speaks of life in his kingdom. That life will never attain perfection on earth; but it is the goal of the believer's striving!

Beware of Hypocrites 6:39–46

Luke classifies this saying as a parable. We will observe (10:25–19:27) that this is a rather loose use of the term. Any moral standing or code of conduct invariably invites hypocrisy (literally: seeming to be something). Words come easily. Deeds speak eloquently. One must be judged by the fruits one produces. The root of all life in the kingdom is the human heart. A heart moved by the Holy Spirit is the good treasury out of which is issued the sound currency of Christian conduct.

Calling Jesus Lord 6:47–49

Coming to Jesus, hearing his words and doing them: that is foundational to confessing Jesus as Lord. A parable drives the lesson home. A true confessor of Christ builds a house upon a foundation laid upon solid rock. When the late fall floods come, that house stands even though torrents of water slap against it. The rock is, of course, Jesus Christ, Rock of Ages. To say that Jesus is Lord involves four things: come to Jesus in faith; build on him for time and eternity; listen to him; follow his directives in word and deed. Blessed is that person who, like Mary of Nazareth, retains and ponders these words in the heart (2:52). And blessed is that person who, like Mary of Bethany, sits at Jesus' feet to keep listening to his word (10:39).

Summary

In the power of the Holy Spirit, Jesus launches his ministry of preaching, teaching, miracles and healing. He early establishes his credentials to speak authoritatively of the kingdom, which God establishes in the life, death, resurrection and glorification of his Son. As Jesus gathers disciples and calls apostles, he faces fierce opposition from the religious rulers who foster an unswerving devotion to the laws handed on from generation to generation. At first very much at home in the synagogue, Jesus encounters an increasingly hostile attitude, which virtually excludes him. This is abetted by his shockingly open stance toward Gentiles, outcasts, women and those usually shunned by a very class-conscious society. At the same time, he carefully inculcates what following him in discipleship entails. Calling Jesus Lord demands no less commitment than that demanded by Pharisees, but stemming form a totally different motivation.

Discussion

1. God's word of law and gospel must be proclaimed. Does where it is proclaimed affect its power to convict of sin and offer grace? Does where it is proclaimed enhance its proclamation?

2. How does the church apply the judgment of Jesus that he is Lord of the Sabbath?

3. Distinguish apostle, disciple and follower. Is it practical to follow Jesus' view of life in his kingdom?

CHAPTER THREE

The Compassion of Christ
Luke 7:1–9:17

Who is this who forgives sins?

The compassion of Christ is extended to persons in truly diverse needs. The portrait of Jesus painted thus far by Luke depicts the Savior as reaching out to diseased, possessed, untouchables, social misfits and religious outcasts. Jesus' ministry of compassion continues to touch a wide spectrum of people experiencing the kind of adversity and suffering, which is common to the human condition.

The Gospel in Word and Deed 7:1–29

As Jesus continues his ministry, both friends and foes are brought closer to the crucial question of his true identity. Is he a great prophet of God? Is he perhaps the Coming One, the long-awaited Messiah? Is he possibly preparing the way for someone else? Is his ministry parochial in nature or does it extend to Jews and Gentiles alike?

For a Caring Gentile 7:1–10

A Roman centurion commanded the local military post. He was a powerful person, someone to be respected, feared and obeyed. This particular centurion was a rarity. He cared about his slave, he had remarkably open attitude toward Jews and he had even built a synagogue for their use. He was a considerate man. Aware of the Hebrew proscription of entering a Gentile house, the centurion does not expect or demand of Jesus what would compromise a strict Jew. In great faith he asks, not orders, Jesus merely to speak a word of healing. A compassionate Christ exclaims that he has not found this kind of faith in all Israel. Gentiles are not excluded from the ministry of our Lord.

For a Grieving Widow 7:11–17

Dr. Luke's diagnosis is that the centurion's servant is completely cured. He employs a normal medical term used of a patient sitting up in a bed when Jesus' life-restoring word is spoken. The lot of widows in that society was far from good. Now this widow is suddenly beret of the sustenance and support of her only son. Jesus happens upon the funeral procession near the city gate where rock tombs were located. Compassion and power are formidable allies. As awe grips the curious crowd who witnessed the miracle, the crowd is moved to glorify God and acclaim Jesus a great prophet. Perhaps the thoughts of many of them go back through the centuries when, in the same area, Elisha raised another mother's son from the dead (2 Kings 4:18–37).

For an Imprisoned Prophet 7:18–29

John is in the dungeon fortress of Herod (so Mark 6:17ff), which served as a prison for his most feared political enemies. John is able to dispatch two disciples to pose the critical question on the minds of so many. In reply, Jesus points to his ministry, reprising his startling message in the synagogue of Nazareth (4:16–30). Jesus IS the Coming One. But his ministry is marked by compassion, not compulsion. The popularly prevailing concept of messianic rule centered in expectation of a warrior messenger of God. His arms would obliterate any force, including Roman legions, which would prevent successful restoration of the throne of David over Israel and perhaps over all nations. The coming Messiah would inaugurate an apocalyptic struggle such as the world had not seen.

People who cannot change warped and wanting notions about the Messiah find in Jesus, not deliverance, but a stumbling block, an occasion of deep offense (2:30–35). The gospel Jesus proclaims is always scandalous to people whose own self-contrived ideas about the way of salvation are cast in concrete. Jesus is God's answer to the problems of human sun, guilt and estrangement. We are not to look for another simply because there is none other.

Jesus' declaration puts John's mind at ease. He is not suffering confinement and isolation because of misplaced or misguided zeal. He is the first-century Elijah who heralds the way of God's Anointed (Malachi 4:5). His ministry is vindicated. Yet paradoxically, those who become part of God's kingdom after him are greater than he. The ultimate fulfillment of the Messiah's ministry is his death and triumphant resurrection.

The Son of Man in Action 7:30–8:48
Compassion is often misunderstood, even outright rejected. God's grace was offered in the ministry of John. Those who heeded his message and received his baptism made a good choice. In contrast, scribes and Pharisees frustrate every effort of God to include them in his kingdom. In his interaction with people, John neither ate nor drank. His austere lifestyle invited harsh criticism. In his social commerce with people, Jesus did eat and drink. His opponents, self-praised paragons of virtue, accuse him of being a gluttonous sot. You can't win when perversity prevails. The wisdom of God in using the ministry of an ascetic and of his own Son is reckoned as just (and wise) by those who in the power of the Spirit actually experience it.

Forgiveness and Faith 7:36–50
It is difficult, if not impossible, correctly to judge motives. Simon, a Pharisee, invites Jesus to dinner. Why he does so remains a moot question. Perhaps he found pleasure in surrounding himself with popular figures of the day. Prominent rabbis were often guests at such affairs and Simon accords Jesus the title, teacher. But Simon feels no need for God's mercy and shows no love for the mercy received. The woman pours out her love in response to her faith in mercy.

This is the second instance related by Luke, which witnesses the Savior's compassion and love (5:18–26). Again the critical question is raised: Who is this who also forgives sins? The question must be answered. In his carefully ordered narrative Luke is leading to that crucial point when the answer is clearly given (9:18–22).

Proclaiming the Good News 8:1–39
Jesus takes his ministry to the open country. Luke describes this phase of it as preaching and announcing the good news in cities and villages. Virtually shut out of the synagogue, Jesus follows the practice of itinerant rabbis. He is accompanied by the Twelve and by certain women

who had experienced his compassionate ministry. A few are named to indicate the diverse company who served Jesus out of their own resources. Mary, from the city of Magdala, is perhaps the unnamed woman at Simon's dinner party. Joanna is the wife of an important finance minister in Herod's government. Of Susanna we know nothing except that she ministered to the Lord. Itinerant teachers were commonly favored with that kind of practical support.

The Lord's proclamation of the good news is likened to sowing seed. What happens to the seed is a spiritual phenomenon described as a secret, or mystery, of the kingdom. Jesus interprets the parable in terms of response. Those who hear the word and cling to the word bear fruits of faith with courage and determination. The apostles are to take note that their own work will meet with similar results. Much may appear to be in vain. But they must not surrender to discouragement or despair. God will always have his harvest.

Possibly as a continuation of his Sermon on the Plain, Jesus shares three pithy logia with the multitudes. The word he sows produces light. It produces openness and honesty. It prompts continuous growth in understanding. The injunction is clear. Take heed to the word! If we fail to grow in faith and the fruits of faith, what we have can be lost. As we retain the word and act according to it, we show ourselves to be the spiritual family of Christ.

Luke inserts two incidents in his narrative, which graphically and vividly depict Jesus as Lord over elements of physical and human nature, which are destructive. Storms often shattered the silence of the sea. In this instance, an unusually violent and terrifying wind causes seasoned fishermen to feel imperiled. As Lord over nature, Jesus stills both wind and wave. The presence in Gerasa of a maniacally man of enormous strength fills the townspeople with terror. The name, legion, deriving from a Roman regiment, indicates the intensity and severity of the derangement. The poor man feels driven by six thousand demons. The Gerasenes witness a marvelous manifestation of mercy and might. Unfortunately it is lost on them because they value material wealth more than the Savior. The man who is cured becomes a dramatic and effective witness to the ministry of Jesus who had delivered him.

The Personal Touch 8:40-56

The Lord whose word calms the disrupting forces of nature and drives out demons of despair is unquestionably Lord over life and death. Jairus is leader of the local synagogue, a position of great respect, honor and authority in the community. His only daughter, on the very brink of physical and cultural adulthood, has been declared dead. Mourners had already gathered in the house to begin the traditional routine of weeping and wailing. Jesus judges differently. Having grasped her hand, he speaks deliberately and directly: Child, rise! The episode of the woman, ostracized on account of ceremonial uncleanness (Leviticus 15:19-33), prompts Dr. Luke to note that she sought a medical cure. But medicine was impotent to restore soundness. In great faith (Deuteronomy 22:12) she experiences the cure she had sought. The compassionate Christ is not only Savior, but Lord as well.

Lessons in Ministry: Success and Failure 9:1-17

Proclamation and power are linked together as Jesus commissions the twelve to carry his ministry to city and village (8:1). They are to go unencumbered by anything that might distract or hinder them from pursuing their specific purpose. If a town refuses their ministry they are to do as Jews did upon leaving Gentile territory. As the apostles shake "heathen" dust off their sandals, it is a poignant sign that a community is rejecting the ministry of Jesus. Their mission must have met with considerable success. For when news comes to Herod – presumably from his spies – the conscience-stricken tetrarch is superstitiously troubled.

As the apostles review their tour with Jesus, he takes them to a fairly remote village north of the Sea of Galilee. This could have been a most welcome and productive time for reflection and review. But multitudes throng about Jesus. This does permit the twelve to witness his own preaching and healing ministry. The miraculous feeding highlights two extremely important truths: Jesus shows compassion for physical as well as for spiritual hunger; the apostles are unable to supply the physical needs of the crowd. Success is tempered by the hard reality of failure. Those who witness the word and serve in the ministry of the church need to be aware of both success and failure. As Jesus distributes the loaves, he looks heavenward and blesses them. A typical

Hebrew prayer at a meal praises God, King of the universe, who causes bread to come forth from the earth.

Summary

In this segment of his narrative, Luke stresses the compassionate ministry of Jesus. The Savior responds to physical and spiritual distress. In word and act he reaches out to teach, touch, heal and restore. His is a ministry from which even the enmity, perversity and misunderstanding of humankind will not deter him. He is being led by the power of the Holy Spirit (4:1, 14–15). He sends out the Twelve, empowering them to preach and heal, that they might experience something of their mission to continue his ministry after his passion and resurrection (24:36–49).

Discussion

1. Does demonic possession belong to a first-century view of the world or is it also a twenty first-century phenomenon?
2. Religion is religion: one is really as good as another.
3. Has the church tended to neglect the healing ministry of Jesus? How can a healing ministry be both abused and neglected?

Conclusion

In his attempt to provide Theophilus with a full and reliable account of the ministry of Jesus, Luke has carefully narrated events from Jesus' birth, baptism and testing, to the inauguration of his ministry in Nazareth. Historical anchorage is provided by linking the birth to a census taken during the reign of Caesar Augustus and the preparatory ministry of John to the reign of Tiberius in Rome and procuratorship of Pilate in Judea. Having set the stage for the ministry of Jesus, Luke clearly and imaginatively sets forth the universal character of his mission. The descent of Jesus is traced to Adam, biblical father of all nations. The voice crying in the wilderness prepares the way of the Lord so that all flesh may see God's salvation. Jesus, the light of revelation to Gentiles, goes out of his way to praise a Gentile centurion's faith. A truly diverse cross-section of society is touched by his ministry. People, who are sick and distressed, be they societal pariahs or paragons, are in need of the care ad cure brought by a physician. Jesus is neither selective nor discriminatory in his outreach to seek and save the lost. Women are accorded a prominent place as Luke intentionally unfolds the drama in which Theophilus will hopefully become more than a mere spectator.

At this point of Luke's account, Jesus also reaches a watershed in his ministry. The apostles must know exactly who he is. More importantly, they must clearly understand who he is. The great confession they are about to make, the Transfiguration on the mountain and the announcement of his impending passion are design to lead them to realize that God's Anointed One will not sweep into power on the waves of revolt and revolution. Jesus will reign as God's King. But the way of the kingdom is passion, cross, death and resurrection.

Part Two

Ministry of
Teaching and Parable

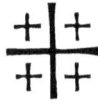

+|+
—+—
+|+

CHAPTER FOUR

Ministry of Teaching
Luke 9:18–10:24

Prophets desired to hear the things you are hearing.

Luke introduces this segment of his narrative with three significant observations: Jesus is at prayer; he prays alone; the disciples are with him. Jesus has reached that plateau of his ministry from which he looks toward Jerusalem and the place of the skill where he is to be crucified (9:51; 23:33). The text provides neither data nor hint as to the content of his prayer. We may surmise that he seeks from his Father vision, determination and strength to carry out his mission to enable God's kingdom come (11:2). In this, Jesus is quite alone. Only one can complete the task set before him. He may be surrounded by milling multitudes, curious crowds and devoted disciples. In traveling the road, which leads to the cross he is always alone. Yet he is sustained by prayer.

Confession and Transfiguration 9:18–36

The disciples have much to learn about Jesus, about the kingdom of God, about themselves as his followers and emissaries. The answer to the critical question posed by Jesus reflects one slice of popular Jewish messianic lore (9:7–9). One who can perform the mighty deeds witnessed in his ministry must be a special prophet raised up by God. Surely the messianic era has dawned (7:16). But Jesus must directly confront his disciples, especially the twelve. You – whom do you hold me to be? Peter's answer is just as direct: the Anointed (Christ) of God! Our Lord's response to this positive confession is as troubling to the readers of the third Gospel as it was to the disciples. Why should Jesus elicit their correct response only to forbid them to announce it? Anticipating their confusion – and attempting to clear up their confusion – Jesus continues: It is absolutely necessary for the Son of Man to suffer, to be rejected, to be killed, to be raised up. None of this fit their notion of messiahship. A precipitous and uninformed messianic movement would incite insurrection and surely lead to a ruinous end. There is no quick and easy way to establish God's kingdom (4:1–13). It must come on God's terms. How much spiritual harm has been done by zealous, but sadly misinformed and misguided, pseudo-witnesses for Christ?

Losing and Saving Life 9:23–27
A disciple is both a learner and a follower. Jesus does not want or need superficial avowals of commitment. People, who do not really know who Jesus is, or what he expects of his followers, are not ready for his kingdom. Christian commitment entails following Jesus, denying one-self in favor of Jesus, readiness to suffer for Jesus and daily dedication to Jesus. True life is not discovered in exaltation of self; it is gained in surrender to Christ. Such loyalty is never misplaced. Those who persist in loyalty to the Son of Man will share in the glory of his Father. In Jesus' own day, many would be able to see the heavenly kingdom break into the earthly realm.

Glory and Affirmation 9:28–36
These strong words must have troubled the disciples even more. He surely is God's Messiah. The Holy Spirit had revealed that to them. But a Messiah who speaks of his own suffering and of losing one's life in his cause? Of what kind of kingdom is he speaking? Messianic armies would incur losses as they routed Roman garrisons out of Israel. Would some of them experience cruelties heaped upon past revolutionaries? Rome was swift to react to revolt with horrible retaliation including mass crucifixions. As they ponder it all, it is possible that they question their confession. Might he after all be just another mixed-up messianic and apocalyptic dreamer? God gives them the answer. On the mount of Transfiguration, while at prayer, Jesus is glorified before their once weary, but now fully opened eyes. The great lawgiver and the great prophet of Israel appear with Jesus. They hear the voice of heavenly ap-probation: Jesus is my beloved Son. You may not comprehend what he is trying to teach you. He may not fit the mold of your messianic ideas. But he is MY Messiah – listen to him! What happened on the mount was so compelling, so overwhelming, they could not even speak of it.

But they knew what they had seen and heard.

Triumph and Greatness 9:37–62
The inner circle of apostles ardently desires to prolong the mountain top experience, recalling the incident with Moses centuries before (Exodus 24). But they must return to the realities of following a Master whose glory is not always easily beheld (9:33).

A Twisted Generation 9:37–45
The father of an epileptic, whose seizures were unusually convulsive (so Dr. Luke), had sought relief from the disciples. They were utterly at a loss as to what to do. Jesus immediately assumes control of a potentially disastrous situation. The crowd is beside itself in awe and wonder. As the multitudes marvel, Jesus again impresses upon the minds (ears) of his disciples that the way to Jerusalem is the way of deliverance into hands, which will crucify him. His saying falls upon unhearing ears (8:10).

Thoughts About the Kingdom 9:45–56
Ideals of a political, earthly kingdom apparently persist. The disciples may not really grasp his references to rejection, suffering and death; they do not understand that in a temporal kingdom Jesus will need able and dedicated cabinet officers. Which among the Twelve should receive the highest appointments? Jesus knows their penchant for power and prestige. Instead of rebuking their misguided aspirations, he places a child next to the king. The one prepared to serve a youngster who has no political power or standing can be counted as greatest. John and his brother James have an even more important lesson to learn. They are not and never will be in control of God's kingdom. They don't have authority to exclude or eliminate someone not of their immediate circle. Neither do they have the power to destroy people, even hated Samaritans, who are not amenable to Jesus' message – a lesson, which his own church frequently failed to remember!

Conversion or Convenience? 9:57–62
Three would-be converts provide context for Jesus to reaffirm the real implications of discipleship. The true follower of Jesus must carefully

count the cost involved. Personal comforts, family duties, distracting loyalties may interfere with the kind of commitment Jesus to reaffirm the real implication of discipleship. The true follower of Jesus must carefully count the cost involved. Personal comforts, family duties, distracting loyalties may interfere with the kind of commitment Jesus requires. At a later time a great church was faulted for its divided allegiances. The writer wishes it were either hot or cold, not luke-warm (Apocalypse 3:14–15).

Woes and Blessings 10:1–24

Jesus' commission to the twelve to proclaim the good news (6:12–19; 9:1–9) is augmented by his appointment of seventy to assist in his own ministry to gather harvest for the kingdom. Seventy were selected to assist Moses in his wilderness ministry (Numbers 11:16–25). Those commissioned by Jesus will not have an easy task, but that is also part of commitment. As they proclaim peace (shalom) many will find wholeness of body and spirit. They will know that the kingdom of God has come to them. Some will not receive it. A frightening responsibility attaches to the ministry of the word. Whenever one hears the word one hears Jesus and the Father who sent him.

The seventy enjoy the sweet taste of success. They see things of which they never dreamed. Nonetheless, their real triumph, their real cause for elation, is the fact that their own names are written in God's book of life. As he reflects on the success of this mission, Luke reminds us that also in this phase of the Lord's ministry, the Holy Spirit is active. In the Spirit, the Son is aware of his unique relationship with the Father. The Son has revealed realities, which were denied the great prophets and kings of Israel. For Jesus Christ is the fulfillment of all prophecies and promises (24:25–27).

Summary

The striving of the compassionate Christ to see and save the perishing continues. Luke places special emphasis on its teaching aspects. Led by the Spirit and undergirded by prayer, Jesus must provide clarification as to his own identity, his role in proclaiming God's reign, the meaning of the kingdom and the essence of discipleship. On two different occasions he announces his rejection by the spiritual leaders of Israel, which leads to suffering, death and resurrection. He permits glimpses of his own divine glory and of the role to be assigned to his apostles and disciples after he has fulfilled the mission assigned by the Father to him. His teaching will continue. But it will increasingly assume the form of parables. Opposition to his ministry worsens and grows as Jesus sharpens the cleavage between the religious establishment and his continuing separation from it. As his public ministry draw to its close, Jesus informs the Twelve for the third recorded time that he will be subjected to cruel and fatal rejection. It will come not only form the leaders of Israel, but from Gentiles as well (18:31–34).

Discussion

1. The Lord can build his kingdom by himself. But he chooses to build it through others.

2. What does it mean for a twentieth century disciple of Jesus to count the cost of confessing Jesus as Lord?

3. Why were there so many false notions as to the kingdom of God and the role of God's Messiah?

CHAPTER FIVE

Ministry of Parables (I)
Luke 10:25–15:32

Happy are those who hear the word of God and keep it.

The continuation of Jesus' ministry increasingly takes the form of teaching by means of parables. Luke includes twenty-seven parables in his account of the events handed down from original sources (1:1–4). Eighteen of them are found only in the third Gospel. Luke's research thus presents a much more complete picture of what many have labeled the Lord's favorite instructional methodology. A parable is simply an illustrative story. Generally it is drawn from normal experiences. The word literally means something laid alongside something else – either for purposes of comparison or contrast. Parable is sometimes used to denote a proverb or particularly pithy saying (4:23). In its proper sense, a parable is usually a consistent narrative, employing simile(s) drawn from earthly things to convey spiritual truth(s).

The interpretation of parables is a challenging undertaking. One must carefully guard against both over and under interpretation. Specific items or details might be fascinating and lead to ingenious comparisons; but they may not at all pertain to the central point of the parable. One is compelled to seek the key thrust of the story in its main point of comparison. In contrast to parable, allegory utilizes metaphor(s). Perhaps the most famous allegory in the Gospels is that found in John 10:1–18, while the most difficult allegory in the New Testament is that found in Galatians 4:21–31.

Love and Prayer 10:25–11:13

The parable of the merciful traveler or good neighbor was prompted by a good question asked for bad reasons. A scribe, trained expert in all matters of Jewish law and tradition, puts Jesus to the test. He asks a classic theological question (Deuteronomy 6:4; Leviticus 19:18). The issue at hand is Jesus' understanding of the term: neighbor.

Parable of the Good Neighbor (Samaritan) 10:25–37

Some interpreters restricted the word, neighbor, to mean only a fellow Jew. Note that the entire dialog deals not with the way to salvation, but with the concept: Who is my neighbor? In his parabolic reply, Jesus selects the most notorious road in the vicinity. It was a tortuous and virtually unprotected lane, which had become a favorite for thieves and thugs. Few would travel the road alone. But Jesus is not discussing the merits or folly of solitary travel. The point is that a half-dying victim of a savage mugging needs a compassionate neighbor. He finds none in a priest or in a Levite, both involved in ritualistic duties in the Temple. The man beaten by bandits finds a good neighbor in the one least likely to be compassionately disposed toward him. The scribe gets the point. This, of course, is also what it means to be a follower of Jesus (8:18, 21).

The Better Part 10:38–42

In an unnamed village (probably Bethany), Jesus and his disciples are hospitably received by two sisters who may have belonged to those who ministered to their needs (8:1–3). Mary listened attentively to the word Jesus was speaking. Martha was busily occupied with serving. Both are engaged in highly commendable pursuits. At this particular time in his ministry, on the way to Jerusalem and the ordeal there awaiting him, Jesus commends Mary. She has chosen the better part of discipleship. Love for Jesus always betokens love of his word.

The Practice of Prayer 1:1–13

Two versions of the prayer taught by Jesus are recorded in the New Testament. The Lukan version is the shorter (Cf. Matthew 6:9–13). The disciples know how to pray. They request a special prayer, which identifies them as followers of Jesus, a common rabbinical practice. The so-called Lord's Prayer – or Our Father – is totally exclusive in that it is for the disciples of Jesus. It is not equally suited to person of any religion or no religion. It is for all who in the power of the Holy Spirit confess Jesus to be Lord. Yet is a totally inclusive prayer. It addresses God, not as King of the universe, which he most certainly is, but as Father whose name reveals grace and mercy. As we reverence God's revelation of his gracious intent to seek and save the perishing, we may pray for the coming of his kingdom, for daily sustenance, for remission of sins and for deliverance from every trial, test and temptation that would separate us from him (9:23–27; 10:21–24).

The parable of the midnight friend demonstrates how Jesus uses the circumstances of custom to illustrate God's willingness to hear prayer. In a typical Jewish village, at midnight the daily supply of bread was gone and doors were closed to indicate that privacy must be respected. Nevertheless, in response to the insistence – really unmitigated persistence – of a friend the door will be opened. Our Father in heaven will open his door to the suppliant. Jesus then uses the circumstance of region to illustrate God's gracious will toward those who seek him in prayer. Smooth stones in that desert area may resemble loaves, snakes may resemble fish, poisonous scorpions may resemble eggs. But what human father would give them to a child requesting food? How much more will God provide good gifts for his children!

Signs and Snares 11:14–12:59
Jesus had resolutely set his face toward Jerusalem, the place of suffering and death (9:20–22, 51). As he pursues his mission to seek and save, opposition is on the rise. It is not limited to elders, chief priests, scribes and Pharisees; the entire generation is wicked because it demands signs, which will ostensibly satisfy its craving curiosity.

The Sign of Jonah 11:14–36
Belief in demonism and various rites of exorcism were rife in Palestine. Opponents launch a three-fold attack on Jesus' ministry of healing. They accuse him of being a functionary of Satan; they try to trap him; and they seek from him a sign for heavenly approval. Jesus meets his adversaries on their own shaky ground. Will the prince of demons assist in expelling his own minions? Furthermore, if exorcists practice their craft in the power of Satan, their own Jewish exorcists stand condemned. Jesus' casting out of demons is a sign that the kingdom has arrived in his ministry. He is conquering Satan, not in league with Satan. Those who see and hear must take a stand. They must declare for Jesus for they are opposed to God's working among them. If they continue to demand signs and set snares to entrap Jesus, they will discover that they are like the person who ends up possessed by seven demons.

The hankering of spiritually restlessness people after sensational signs, portents and omens is symptomatic of a deep spiritual sickness. Its cure is found in Jesus' retort to the woman caught up in the emotion of the moment: Happy are they who hear the word of God and retain it! Jonah proclaimed the word to pagan Nineveh and the Queen of Sheba came to hear the word and wisdom of Solomon. Jesus is greater than both Jonah and Solomon; and his own generation accuses him of being in league with Satan. Such a generation can only expect judgment. Jesus is the light of humankind, the eye, which admits God's light. Without that, all is spiritual darkness. Seeking signs and setting snares is like putting God's light in the cellar or under a basket that none may see the glow of God's grace.

Fools and Hypocrites 11:37–12:12

Elaborate rituals for washing the hands assured punctilious observance of traditional ceremonial cleanness. Equally elaborate laws concerning tithes and offerings assured proper religious standing. Occupying chief seats in the synagogue assured proper honor in the community. Externals have a place in devotion. The offering of tithes and first fruits of all growing things was a powerful and constant reminder that the earth belongs to the Lord (Psalm 24). He opens his hands to sustain life and grant daily provision (11:3). But traditionalists all too often substituted external acts and observances for love of God and concern for social justice. Their inner spiritual being was corrupt; and they corrupted those with whom they came into contact (Numbers 19:16). Religion is not always beneficial. False religion can be more harmful than no religion.

As the teachers of the law excoriate Jesus for his disrespectful treatment of the Pharisees, Jesus condemns them for their own hypocrisy. They delight in constructing intricately detailed rules and codes of daily conduct. But they always find ways to excuse themselves from the burdens they impose on others. They erect lavish and ornate monuments to the prophets who are dead. At the same time, they persecute the living prophets. They purport to be privileged sons of the kingdom. In reality, they keep people out of the kingdom with their extreme legalism. The reaction of both scribes and Pharisees is to set even greater snares to entrap Jesus and level charges against him.

With an eye toward historical detail, Luke records that myriads – people by the thousands – gather to hear Jesus. He warns against those who are merely action out of religious roles, putting masks as Greek tragedians did on the stage. Hypocrisy can easily come across as conviction and sincerity. That makes it all the more dangerous. Luke incorporates certain logia, which may well be part of the Sermon on the Plain. No human power, not even ecclesiastical authority to the God who reaches out to humankind in the ministry of the Son of Man is our paramount spiritual priority. God sends his Holy Spirit to enlighten and lead the lost and perishing to Jesus Christ. If one continually rejects every overture of the Spirit by attributing divine works to demons, that person commits what is usually called the unforgivable sin. Did the hypocrisy of the Pharisees come close to that? On that other hand, those summoned before a religious tribunal to give an account of their faith in Jesus Christ as Lord and Savior are not to fear. The Holy Spirit will teach them what to say in their defense.

Signs of the Times 12:13–59

Rabbis and revered teachers often served as referees in family disputes. Jesus uses an incident to warn against greed and a totally false sense of values. The parable of the rich fool is intended to give possessions their rightful place in the scheme of things. Jesus returns to this theme in the parable of the crafty steward (16:1–13). A wise person masters his possessions and never puts his trust in them. A fool is mastered by his possessions because he puts his trust in them. If the grace of God is our real treasure, our heart will cling to that above all else. Therefore, strive for the kingdom of God! Put that first in your life. For it is God's good pleasure to give his kingdom to those who seek it. Such seeking must also be constant.

The parable of he happy servant (12:35–40) stresses the absolute necessity of watchful preparation. For the end may come at any moment. The wick of the lamp must be kept trimmed. The tail of the work-robe must be tucked into the girdle so one is not hampered.

The parable of the faulty servant (12:36–48) is a powerful reminder that one must exercise vigilant control over one's God-given goods. The fool believes that he is totally unaccountable in the use, care and disposition of the gifts bestowed by a gracious Lord.

A radically altered attitude toward wealth and possessions is a sign of the true messianic age, that the kingdom has indeed come in the ministry of Jesus (11:20). Another sign is the radical alteration of social and family ties, which the kingdom causes. The Jews regarded fire as a symbol of judgment. Metaphorically understood, a baptism (not the technical sense of sacrament) signified an immersion in a radically reoriented cause. Jesus will undergo such a baptism. His passion, death and resurrection will be a totally shattering experience for people whose expectation of a golden messianic era was one of total peace. In the early life of the church, political and social structures, including families, were often subjected to terrible tensions on account of tested loyalty and commitment to Christ.

People within the sphere of Jesus' ministry had asked for signs (11:29). Jesus is providing one sign after another. They are far different from the kind of demanded by the multitudes. They can read meteorological signs; they cannot read theological signs. Yet there is an urgency for them to do so. One in the crowd surrounding Jesus had asked him to serve as judge in a matter of probate (12:13). This request becomes a sign of status before God. In God's court the people will lose their case because they are guilty. There fore they must come to terms with the situation now, while there is still time. Jesus may not have come bearing earthly peace. But he most assuredly has come to bring peace with God, the peace of which the angel sang in praising God for the gift of the Savior who is Christ the Lord (2:8–14).

Repentance and the Kingdom 13:1–15:32

How does one make peace with the heavenly Judge? Jesus states it unambiguously: Unless you repent you will all perish!

The Reality of Sin 13:1–17

By means of two incidents peculiar to the third Gospel, Luke addresses the ever-contemporary issue of the reality and gravity of sin. The religious leaders of the day were prone to link sin and suffering. It follows that they weighed the seriousness of sins on the scale of infractions of their laws and traditions. The first incident was especially heinous because it involved the Roman governor who took drastic measures against some Galileans who opposed his policy. That may help explain why Pilate had a tenuous relationship with Herod (23:6–12). Less is known regarding the Siloam disaster. The unnamed delegation, which confronted Jesus, obviously reflected the attitude that the unfortunate victims must have been super-sinners. Jesus uses the occasion to call for repentance. Instead of attempting to measure the gravity of certain sins, they must repent of their own sins. As he issues the stern warning and summons, he quite likely has an even greater disaster in mind; the utter destruction of Jerusalem and its Temple (21:21–24).

The parable of the fig tree demonstrates another fact of the reality of sin. God's people are to produce fruits of faith, which glorify him. God is extremely patient. Yet Patience has an end. Sins of omission also have their time of judgment. The healing performed by Jesus on a Sabbath was, to the mind of strict and rigorous interpreters of the law, a most grievous sin. Work violated the sanctity of the Sabbath. Referring to their own practices, Jesus considers mercy to a daughter of Abraham to be more important. Their hypocrisy is the greater sin.

Entering the Kingdom 13:18–14:35

The adversaries of Jesus were confident that they were in God's kingdom. They – and scarcely anyone else! They were not only sons of Abraham; they were zealous exponents, protectors and practitioners of the traditions of their fathers. They knew precisely to what they would compare the kingdom. But to what will Jesus compare it? In Palestine the mustard seed often grew to unusual heights. The kingdom of God is much bigger and broader than the scribes and Pharisees ever imagined. Even Gentiles have a place in it. The kingdom may have small beginnings, but it grows and spreads like leaven without human limitation. The Jews envisioned the kingdom as their own special domain. Luke sees the kingdom as embracing all who will enter it by repentance and faith. Those who think that the door of salvation is closed to everyone else will tragically discover that it is closed to them. Abraham, Isaac and Jacob – bearers of the covenant promise – will indeed be in the kingdom. But with them, at the messianic feast of salvation, will be the many who come from the ends of the world. They are the ones who in the day of opportunity and gracious invitation strive (literally: struggle) to enter the kingdom on God's terms, not their own. Jerusalem (Israel) was given prophet after prophet to warn the people of the covenant to be faithful to God's gracious promises. In willful obstinacy, they stoned the servants of God, closing their ears to all his pleas.

Some Pharisees, perhaps genuinely friendly to Jesus, warned him of Herod's intention. Jesus must warn the Pharisees of even greater peril to themselves. Since Sabbath regulations were such a neuralgic issue with his adversaries, Jesus performs another healing on that sacred day (4:38; 6:5; 13:13). All food consumed on a Sabbath had to be cooked the day before. In addition to ritualistic preparation and preservation of food, rules pertaining to preservation of life on the Sabbath were rigorously enforced. Luke tells us that the guests were carefully scrutinizing Jesus. They may have purposely arranged the whole episode to test Jesus. In spite of that, Jesus heals the man. The kingdom of God does not consist of endless lists of petty practices. Nor does it consist in occupying chief seats in the synagogue (11:40) or at wedding feasts. God's kingdom is characterized by humility and eager readiness to enter it upon the Lord's gracious invitation. When that invitation is at hand, nothing must stand in the way, not family ties, personal possessions or responsibilities. The grand banquet of salvation will not be without guests. The crucial question always remains: Will I be one of them? Then will I be a disciple who can be likened to salt, which helps preserve an age, which is perishing in its own corruption? Entering and remaining in the kingdom of God has highest priority in life. Whoever has an ear to hear, let that person hear and heed what the Savior clearly inculcates: Unless you repent you will perish (13:5).

Repentance and Acceptance 15:1–32

Pharisees and scribes substituted rejection for repentance. Simply stated, they felt they needed no repentance for themselves. They indignantly rejected any notion of repentance as it was proclaimed by John the Baptizer and Jesus. And there were some to whom an offer of repentance and restoration must not be extended. Chief among them were the despised tax-collectors and a host of people whom the Pharisees neatly gathered under the umbrella bearing the bright label: sinners. They were so designated because they made neither effort nor pretense of observing the laws and traditions of the elders. To the Pharisaic mind, they were beyond the pale of social interaction and spiritual redemption. Yet Jesus associated with them. He even broke bread with them. In so doing, he disregarded all of their social, cultural and spiritual taboos.

The parables of the rejoicing shepherd, the seeking woman and the loving father emphasize how precious in the sight of God is each person who repents and finds acceptance with God. Instead of rejection there is acceptance. The message of the gospel is clear: Jesus came to seek and to save the perishing. When the lost are found and restored by a gracious God and Father, there must be joy in place of murmuring. A lost sheep, a lost coin and lost son have a place in the kingdom of God, which is not shared by those who self-deceptively imagine they need no repentance and who self-righteously begrudge repentance to those who realize they need it.

Summary

Luke has incorporated in his narrative a number of parables, which are not found in other Gospels. In this segment are included the parable of the compassionate Samaritan (10:25), the midnight friend (11:5), the rich fool (12:13), the fruitless tree (13:6), the foolish builder (14:28), the imprudent king (14:30), the lost coin (15:8) and the forgiving father (15:11). Luke employs parables to accent basic differences between the religious leaders and Jesus with regard to the kingdom of God. Jesus attempts to penetrate the wall of theology built to restrict the saving grace of God. Luke stresses the divine love, which reaches out to Jews, Samaritans and Gentiles alike. This note of universalism is particularly appropriate as Luke writes for Theophilus and as the church is reaching out to evangelize non-Jews as well as Jews. At the same time, Luke traces the reasons for the growing antagonisms, which peak in the ultimate separation of the religious establishment from the messianic ministry and mission of Jesus. As he continues his ministry of parables, Jesus will speak out even more pointedly of the true nature of God's kingdom and what it mean to become a part of it.

Discussion

1. Is the distinction between sins of commission and omission, mortal and venial, a valid one?

2. What in the contemporary church can become a substitute for genuine repentance?

3. Why was a mission to Gentiles so offensive to the Jews of the first century?

CHAPTER SIX

Ministry of Parables (II)
Luke 16:1–19–27

Today salvation has come to this house.

Jesus still pursues the path, which inescapably leads to his stated goal: Jerusalem, where he will encounter mockery and maltreatment, condemnation and crucifixion (9:44; 18:31–32). Prior to his triumphal celebration on Palm Sunday, Jesus has much to impart to the multitudes, the disciples and his apostles. In Luke's arrangement of the didactic material drawn from his sources, parables constitute a major witness to the Lord's ministry. The parables of the dishonest steward (16:1), Dives and Lazarus (16:19), the dutiful servant (17:7), the robber judge (18:1) and the Pharisee and tax-collector (18:9) are unique to the third Gospel. In addition, the story of Zacchaeus, found in this segment and which provides the theme of the Gospel (19:1), is peculiar to Luke.

The Peril of Possessions 16:1–17:10

Material possessions and prosperity are not per se to be condemned out of hand as intrinsically evil. Not money, but the love of money, is the root of all evil.

God or Mammon 16:1–18

Mammon was the name given to possessions, which had become a god to the possessor. The parable is quite detailed in its unfolding of the machinations of its various characters. All appear to be unsavory. The point of comparison in the parable is, by contrast, simple and straightforward: You cannot be a server of God and Mammon, just as no household slave can serve two different masters at the same time. A slave was obligated to serve his master with undivided zeal and obedience. He could not moonlight on the side. Loyalty and love for God calls for nothing less. Children of the light (believers) can learn a valuable lesson from the clever, but dishonest, steward of the parable. His absolute determination to accomplish a goal, his wisdom and efforts expended to achieve his goal, are worthy of our emulation. The dishonesty and injustice involved are not. We are stewards of all the gifts and possessions God grants us. We are accountable to God for them. Possessions and prosperity may not be sinful per se; they do carry with them a truly awesome responsibility.

Upon hearing the parable, and Jesus' interpretation of it, the Pharisees present laugh him to scorn. Inordinately fond of their wealth, they viewed worldly prosperity as a divine sign of their goodness. And their alleged goodness stemmed, of course, from their devoted observance of their laws and traditions. Jesus uses the opportunity to remind the Pharisees that the word of God, mediated through the law and prophets, held sway until he himself proclaimed the good news, the gospel of the kingdom. The genuine law of God, stripped clean of the thousand and one-minute proscriptions and prescriptions appended to it, is valid (18:18–20; 10:25–27). Jesus perfectly fulfilled the law of God on our behalf. Jesus cites one example of the law's continuing validity (Deuteronomy 24:1). Through the centuries, rabbis and exegetical specialists had tampered with the simple stipulation. In our Lord's time, divorce was sought and obtained because a wife overcooked her husband's dinner.

Rich and Poor 16:19–31

If the Pharisees fail to understand what Jesus is attempting to convey, they miss the earnest warning against misuse of God's blessings. The parable of the rich man (Latin: Dives) is intended to put both riches and stewardship of riches in proper perspective. Wealth was largely measured in terms of land, crops, cattle, buildings, clothing and feasting (Cf. 12:13–34). Dives apparently had it all. Moreover, he had it in abundance since he feasted sumptuously everyday, even on the Sabbath. Lazarus (Hebrew: God is my help) is dirt poor and pitiably ill with ulcerated sores (so Dr. Luke). At death, Lazarus is borne to glory. In spite of his earthly misery, he was a faithful son of the covenant promise. Dives is in hell (Hades, torment), not because he was rich, but because he utterly failed to use his possessions to show mercy, alleviate human misery and love his neighbor. Too late he comes to his senses. His sudden desire to become a missionary is met with the simple truth: They have the word of God. The warning is piercing. Listen to the word! Heed the word now! The allusion to one rising from the dead is surely predictive of Jesus' own mission and ministry of the word (9:22; 18:33).

Scandals and Duty 17:1–10

Sin is a sad and tragic reality of human existence. It is an abomination in the eyes of God no matter who commits it or under what circumstance it occurs. Certain logia of Jesus, possibly drawn from his Sermon on the Plain, are cited by Luke to round out this section of warnings. One very strong saying relates to people who set snares by putting stumbling blocks to sin in the paths of others, even children (9:46–48). Those guilty of baiting people to sin come in for most serious censure. Furthermore, imperfect people in the kingdom of God realize their constant need for repentance and forgiveness, form God and from each other. Jewish tradition spoke of forgiving someone three times. Jesus more than doubles that, not to provide a spiritual calculator, but to emphasize the need to go beyond what human standards may dictate.

Jesus returns to the mustard seed (13:18–19) to illustrate the nature of faith. The apostles apparently are acutely aware of their need for a strong, unwavering trust in Jesus' word. By use of hyperbole, Jesus stresses the qualitative character of faith. It is absolute trust, a trust that persists in spite of any and all obstacles.

Finally, Luke records a logion, which may well sum up our Lord's statements regarding servants, stewards and slaves (16:1–13). Faithful stewards and servants we must be. But the most faithful and loyal must still confess their unworthiness. God calls us into his kingdom. God calls us to responsible stewardship by his grace and by grace alone. One does not respond to God's summons by imagining that such a response somehow puts God in debt to the servant. God claims us on the basis of the life, death and resurrection of his Son. Faith claims God as the God of grace and salvation. But faith never makes a claim on God!

Faith and the Kingdom 17:11–18:30

The kind of faith to be found in God's kingdom reveals itself in countless ways. In carefully crafting this section of his Gospel, Luke permits us to view and reflect on some of them.

Gratitude and Watchfulness 17:11–18:8

Headed toward Jerusalem, in a village on the border, which lies between Galilee and Samaria, Jesus confronts a colony of ten lepers, one of whom is Samaritan. Laws regarding leprosy, feared and nearly always fatal disease of the day, were explicit (Leviticus 13:45–46; Numbers 5:2). Jesus heeds their pitiful pleas. In reaction to his compassion, only one glorifies God and profusely thanks Jesus for healing and restoration to health, family and society. Faith brings spiritual healing. It must also engender gratitude.

The Pharisees were concerned about signs (11:29). The kingdom does not come accompanied by the kind of signs one can study, as a physician checks symptoms of certain diseases. God's kingdom is among them, in their midst. But they can't discern it. Jesus is God's unique revelation. He is God's great sign that the kingdom has been ushered in (4:14–30).

The followers of Jesus will also be concerned about signs. As he frequently does, Jesus, the master Teacher, uses an incident as a springboard to discuss a related issue. The Son of Man will suffer and be subjected to rejection by his own generation. But his very rejection by humankind will be rejected by God in the vindication and triumph of the resurrection and the entrance of Jesus into his glory (24:26, 50–53). In glory, the Son of Man will come again. The day of the Lord's return has been designated by God, unknown to any human being. In spite of that, some will claim to possess secret signs and revelations of the Lord's return. Jesus warns with unmistakable clarity: Disregard all such persons, all such claims and all such so-called signs. But be alert! As the world waits, many will forget the admonition to watch. In the days of Noah and Lot (Genesis 6–19) people ignored the warnings. They became so involved in day by day living that they failed to listen to God. That can happen in any age. If that occurs in the day of Christ's return, only spiritual disaster can follow.

People of faith will, therefore, be ever vigilant. The Lord "will come to judge the living and the dead." But he will come in God's time. Sighs, signs, speculations and suspicions of his coming will not change that. The proverb cited by Jesus merely reiterates his words. The Son of Man comes when conditions laid down by God have been met. He comes according to God's clock, not ours.

The watchfulness mandated by Jesus is to be accompanied by unflagging prayer. The parable of the robber judge (a political appointee who dispensed justice based on bribery) demonstrates the necessity of constant, ceaseless prayer. God is certainly not a robber judge. But if an unjust jurist succumbs to persistent petitions – for whatever reasons – how much more will God hear the pleas of his watchful, waiting people (11:13). God will vindicate his own if we but persist. That is the kind of faith Jesus must find when he returns.

Confession and Humility 18:9–14

The Pharisees could easily describe the kingdom of God (13:18–21) and supply signs for its ultimate coming (17:20). All they had to do was examine their own lifestyle. Praying, fasting, going to the Temple, keeping separate from the rest of humankind: these would rank high in their vocabulary of comparisons and indicators. Prayer was considered to be particularly potent if offered in the sacred precincts of the Temple, to which the proud and pious Pharisee would resort at the appointed hours: 9 A.M., noon and 3 P.M.. Fasting was actually required only Yom Kippur, the solemn day of atonement. Tithes of produce were mandated by the law (Numbers 18:21; Deuteronomy 14:22). They were contributed for the support of Levites and priests. In addition, first fruits of the earth were offered in the Temple. Pharisees often went far beyond the requirements (11:41–42).

The Pharisee in the parable was one of them. So he was totally self-confident as to his righteousness before God. In his self-righteousness he despised the rest of the people. The tax collector, one of the despised, was not only humble before God. He confessed that he was a (Greek: the) sinner and could only beg for mercy. He was acquitted of his sin. He humbled himself before God and was exalted by God with the assurance of forgiveness. All the good things the Pharisee practiced (except his praying, not to God, but with himself) could be commended if done from the right spirit. But he trusted in his deeds for acceptance by God. True faith is marked by humility and expresses itself in recognition and confession of sin.

Trust and Discipleship 18:15–30

Eager mothers customarily brought small children to a rabbi for blessing. For reasons known only to them, the disciples attempt to dissuade them. Jesus not only receives the children he sets them forth as examples of the kingdom. They quality of childlike – not childish – faith is a paradigm for all faith. The trust of the small child is absolute.

The rich young rule fails the test of faith and discipleship. He was apparently serious in his intent to learn. He even approached Jesus as Good Master, an extremely rare form of address among Jews. But Jesus quickly dismantles his façade of religiosity. The ruler almost condescendingly claims he has from his youth kept the commandments of God. Jesus does not argue the case. He directs the man to do the one thing that reveals the true condition of his heart. The ruler loves his riches more than God. He has not kept the law at all! Wealth had become his god (12:13–34; 16:19–31). Having such a god excludes one from entering the kingdom. The apostles are suddenly concerned about their own status in the kingdom. Jesus assures his disciples of every age that one who is ready to commit one's life to the kingdom of God never really loses anything. Faith not only trusts Christ for salvation. Faith opens the kingdom now and is blessed with everlasting life in the age to come.

On the Way to Jerusalem 18:31–19:27

On the way to Jerusalem (17:11) and the cross, Jesus delivers his third and final prediction of his passion. For this momentous announcement, Jesus gathers the apostles about him. He directs them to ponder the mission and ministry foretold through prophetic writings. Luke makes a threefold comment. They understand nothing of these things; this word is hidden from them; they do not grasp the meaning of the sayings. The bald truth of his passion, death and resurrections is at the moment incomprehensible to them.

Jesus, Son of David 18:35–43

Jericho was a prosperous city located in the Jordan valley some seventeen miles from Jerusalem. As Jesus, accompanied by pilgrim bands on their way to celebrate the Passover, approaches the city, a blind man "sees" in Jesus what most of the multitudes – and perhaps even the disciples – fail to see. Jesus of Nazareth is the Messiah who stems from the royal line of Israel (1:30–33; 2:4,11; 20:41–44). The man shouts the designation out. As people at the head of the crowd attempt to silence him, the blind man cries out more vehemently. His is an example of the tenacity of faith. He knows who Jesus is. He believes firmly that Jesus can heal. In response to mercy received, he glorifies God and joins the pilgrim throng on the way.

Salvation Has Come 19:1–10

On the way through Jericho, an important tax center of the district, the chief collector of revenues was seeking also to see Jesus. Zacchaeus had been eminently successful in his profession. He had obviously been made aware of Jesus' compassionate ministry to the despised and the outcasts of society (5:27–32; 18:13–14). The Savior does not disappoint him. Jesus brings salvation to Zacchaeus, for he came to seek and save the perishing. In gratitude and confession, Zacchaeus makes restitution for his fraudulent practices. In so doing, he goes far beyond that required by Hebrew law (Deuteronomy 6:5; Numbers 5:7). In addition he makes a generous contribution to the less fortunate. In faith he knows how to be a good steward (Cf. 16:19–31; 18:18–30). He understands what it means to enter the kingdom of God.

Near Jerusalem 19:11–27

Luke concludes this section, in which he traces the Lord's path on the way to Jerusalem, with another parable. It is addressed to the throngs following Jesus into the city. In true and accepted rabbinic style, Jesus teaches as he travels. The multitudes are intently listening "to these things." Luke observes that Jesus speaks this particular parable for two basic reasons: He was near Jerusalem; the people fully expected (their concept of) the kingdom to appear at once.

The parable may relate, at least in part, to a well-known political situation. Upon his death, Herod, misnamed the Great, divided his kingdom among Antipes (Galilee and Perea), Philip (Ituraea) and Arche-laus (Judea and Samaria). Archelaus was subsequently removed in favor of a Roman procurator (3:1–6). To a people who were so anxious to have Jesus declare his kingship, presumably at the Passover Feast, Jesus would say: Haven't you learned your lesson about kings? Your puppet princes have been less than paragons of virtue and power, especially in Judea. Your revolts against Roman rule have proved disastrous. Yet you want me to claim the throne of David and vanquish in the name of God every Roman garrison stationed in what was once all Israel?

There is deeper significance in the fact that Jesus relates this parable at this time of his ministry. Jesus IS the messianic king. He has come to proclaim God's kingdom. His kingdom entails for him suffering, rejection, death and resurrection. The kingdom of God is entered via repentance and faith. Faith produces the fruits of which Jesus has been speaking. His antagonists and adversaries do not want this kind of messianic king. But those who do want to enthrone him in their hearts and lives will be faithful stewards and servants. They will also learn that the law of the kingdom is always operable. Those who are faithful will experience the greatest blessings and rewards (18:28–30).

Summary

Jesus is winding down his teaching ministry. A good part of it has taken the form of parables. For this portion of his narrative, Luke selects five parables, which are not cited by the other evangelists. He also relates the miraculous healing of the ten lepers and the story of Zacchaeus, both of which appear only in this third Gospel. His careful investigations have thus given the church materials which otherwise would have remained unrecorded. Once again we begin to appreciate why the witness of Luke to the ministry of Jesus has been described as the most comprehensive.

Luke's central aim in this segment is to provide glimpses of the kingdom of God and human characteristics that are found in it, but can also exclude from it. Pride, spiritual self-righteousness, love of wealth, unfaithful stewardship of God's gifts, abuse and misuse of the law of God are just some of the barriers which stand in the way. Repentance, confession of sin, humility, faith, a readiness to be found in those who belong to the kingdom. Furthermore, the kingdom is open to

all: Samaritans, Gentiles, those classified as notorious sinners and despised outcasts. Climax of the events recorded by Luke is the dialog
between Jesus and Zacchaeus. The Lord proclaims the unparalleled
good news of salvation. It has come because the Son of Man came to
seek and save the perishing. Of our prayers, Jesus states: Seek and you
will find. Of his ministry he declares: I came to seek and find the lost.

Discussion

1. Is Holy Scripture sufficient to lead us to eternal salvation? Or do
   we need special signs, revelations or esoteric teachings?

2. Do poverty or wealth in and of themselves open or close the door
   of heaven? What dangers attach to both?

3. Do people still misunderstand or fail to grasp the true nature of
   the kingdom of God? Cite contemporary examples.

Conclusion

Our Lord's ministry of teaching and parable has led him from the confession of the Apostles that he is God's Anointed to the hour of his entry into Jerusalem where he will be acclaimed as the blessed King who comes in the name of the Lord. In this part of his witness to the ministry of Jesus, Luke points to the importance of prayer. He accents qualities of faith to be found in disciples of Jesus as he sets them forth in sharp contrast to the hypocrisy, shallowness and obsessive legalism of the scribes and Pharisees.

The materials incorporated by Luke in this section contain three miracle narratives and thirteen parables, which are unique to his account, an indicator as to why, of the Four Gospels, that of Luke has the broadest sweep. Four of these parables feature truly striking personalities: the compassionate Samaritan, the rich fool, Dives and Lazarus, the Pharisee and tax collector. Jesus' hearers would easily recognize each. Three of them center on customs or practices; the friend who comes at midnight, the robber judge, the dishonest steward. Each provides rich background for striking contrasts between human and divine action.

The three clear predictions of the passion and a fourth somewhat veiled one (12:49–50), are intended to demonstrate the Lord's firm resolve to fulfill his ministry to see and save. At the same time, they demonstrate vividly the inability of his closest companions, at the time, to grasp the ultimate goal and meaning of his mission. As Luke continues his narrative, we stand at the final week of our Lord's earthly life. From the Mount of Olives he descends to receive from multitudes accolades of praise, which will soon turn into shouts of accusation and condemnation.

Part Three

Ministry of Tragedy and Triumph

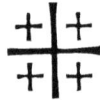

+|+
+|+

CHAPTER SEVEN

Ministry of Fulfillment
Luke 19:28–23:56

Tell us if you are God's Anointed!

Luke's witness to the earthly ministry of Jesus includes a fairly detailed account of the final week of that ministry. While all the Gospels grant proper prominence to the final days of our Lord's passion, Luke fleshes out the passion narrative with several specific details not incorporated in the witness of Matthew, Mark and John. The special sources from which Luke the historian has drawn include materials dealing with the disciples (22:24–34), the political charge against Jesus and trial before Herod (23:2–16), the suffering Savior's directive to the weeping women (23:26–31) and three logia spoken from the cross (23:34, 43, 46). Of particular note and significance are the narratives, which relate to the resurrection of our Lord. Luke alone provides information about Easter afternoon (24:13–35), appearances of the Risen Lord in Jerusalem (24:36–49) and the ascension from Bethany (24:50–53). With his acute historical eye for detail, Luke has recovered for the church's promulgation of the good news and the Christian Faith with a considerable wealth of material, which otherwise may have been obscured or permanently lost.

In the Name of the Lord 19:28–48

The final week begins with the joyous celebration the church has come to call the triumphal entry of Palm Sunday. Jesus leaves Jericho for Bethany from which his minutely planned ride is to begin. In the name of Jesus the disciples procure not a horse, symbol of conquering power, but an ass, symbol of peace. In deliberately fulfilling the words of Zechariah (9:9) Jesus proclaims his coming as God's Anointed. The people sense the connection. For they acclaim him the blessed King who in the name of the Lord comes bearing heavenly peace (2:8ff). Yet Jesus must temper his own joy with the sorrow he feels over the city, which is destined to suffer total devastation (21:5–24).

Jesus first enters the holy city. He next enters his holy Temple. From the truly magnificent view of the city afforded the viewer from the Mount of Olives, Jesus goes to the staggeringly magnificent Temple, refurbished and rebuilt by Herod as a gesture of solidarity with the Jews. Jesus rids the Temple of the changers of money and vendors of animals who were practicing their trade. Both businesses were legitimate; but they routinely cheated the people. Worshippers were obligated to exchange currency for sanctuary shekels. Animals for sacrifice could be brought but it was much more convenient to purchase them on site. The Temple shops were controlled by families of the High Priest who victimized pilgrims who had come for worship. The House of God was being profaned in the very name of religion!

As Jesus taught in the colonnades of the Temple, the leaders determined more resolutely to be rid of him once and for all. Ever attuned to the changing moods of the people, they could not make their move until they had a clear accusation to bring against him and his ministry.

Condemnations and Warnings 20:1–21:37
As Jesus pursued his mission, he increasingly sharpened lines of demarcation between himself and his antagonists. The conflict comes to a head when the authorities directly challenge Jesus and his teachings. The questions proffered raise delicate and often explosive issues. Design of the questions is entrapment. His enemies need provocation for moving to arrest him and deliver him over for trial and condemnation.

Cite Your Authority 20:1–21:4
Chief priests, scribes and elders, members of the supreme council of the Jews known as the Sanhedrin, pose the first question recorded by Luke. Jesus has on numerous occasions ignored the authority of the council. Most recently he defied their authority by entering Jerusalem as a prophet-king and by cleansing the Temple. Now he is teaching in the Temple area a message, which questions their own interpretation of their laws and traditions. They ask him to cite his authority. If he claims messianic authority, which they fully expect him to do – or,

better yet, if he claims to be the Son of God – they will have a capital accusation: blasphemy. In rabbinic style, Jesus questions them. If John the Baptizer had the authority of God behind his witness to Jesus, the issue is settled. For John clearly taught he was a herald of the Coming One.

The parable spoken by Jesus is a cutting indictment (Isaiah 5:1–7). The religious leaders of Israel maltreated God's prophets who warned the people and called them to repentance and faithful stewardship. They are about to kill God's own Son. God's patience is about to give way to judgment. Changing the metaphor from vineyard to building, Jesus cites Psalm 118:22–23. He is the chief stone in God's spiritual Temple, the church.

His adversaries did not fail to get the message. They were ready to seize him then and there. But they needed something to convince the Roman authorities that Jesus was a rebellious antagonist and threat to Roman rule. So spies interrogate Jesus regarding the onerous annual poll tax of one denarius. All Jews hated the tax. So it was an extremely clever stratagem. The answer Jesus gave foiled their attempts at entrapment. It squared with the realities of political life in the Empire. If Caesar is king and you use his currency, then you must pay the tax. It's as simple as that. There is, however, that realm of life and spirit where Caesar dare not rule. The early church taught loyalty to the state. But it always tempered its teaching with the injunction to fear, honor and obey God above any human institution.

Next in line to snare Jesus by their astuteness are the professional theological sophisticates who feel qualified to challenge him. The sect of Sadducees had no problem with the question of tribute to Caesar. They enjoyed a comfortable relationship with Rome. But they differed markedly with the Pharisees, especially on the doctrine of the resurrection of the dead. Limiting their canon of Scripture and authority to the Pentateuch, more specifically to Torah, the Mosaic Law, they claimed to find no support for such teaching. On the more practical level they wanted no one with messianic visions to upset their rulership over the Temple and its lucrative sources of income. The fabricated case is meant to sound utterly ridiculous, even though based on the so-called levirate law (Deuteronomy 25:5). Jesus deftly replies that in the resurrection age, life is totally different. But Jesus makes clear that there will be a resurrection. Meeting the Sadducees on their own turf, Jesus cites a well-known passage from the Pentateuch (Exodus 3:1–6). God is the God of the living! There will be a resurrection.

When some of the scribes present feel constrained to compliment Jesus on his retort, the Lord turns to them. They are supposed to be experts in interpreting the law. Furthermore, they recognize the authority of the Psalter, popularly ascribed to Davidic authorship. Psalm 110:1 provided an honored messianic title (18:38–39). The Anointed is David's son, that, a royal descendant. But David writes that the Anointed is actually his own Lord. The Anointed (Christ: Messiah) is both son and Lord to David. The scribes, as well as the people, must reorder their ideas about the Messiah, his identity and his role.

The scribes are questioning the authority of Jesus. They demonstrate their own authority by means of various external acts of pseudopiety. Their pretense and hypocrisy are in for severe condemnation. They also reveal their unbridled greed as they prey upon the more vulnerable in their society. Rabbis were supposed to teach without fee, for they had other means of livelihood. But they loved to claim that financial support of their instruction is an act of great merit. Jesus contrasts this with the genuine sacrifice of a poor widow. The scribes trumpeted their religiosity. Her gift of two lepta represented real piety.

Day of Catastrophe 21:5–24

The Temple planned by King David and erected by his son and successor, Solomon, was utterly destroyed in 586 B.C. during the so-called Babylonian Captivity (606–536 B.C.). It was rebuilt upon the return of many of the captives to Jerusalem. The profanation and desecration, as well as looting, of the Temple by the Syrian ruler, Antiochus, some three hundred years later fomented the Maccabeean revolt, which gave Israel a period of political independence. Refurbished and enlarged by Herod, the Temple of our Lord's times was a truly splendid structure. Its marble pillars, cloisters and colonnades presented an awesome sight. While some were admiring the beauty of the Temple, Jesus speaks at length of its devastating, horrible destruction (Cf. 19:41–44).

Jesus uses language reminiscent of the catastrophe of 586 B.C., a never to be forgotten incident on Jewish history. Interwoven in his predictive discourse regarding the Temple are strands of prophecy dealing with his own return. He speaks of both in language couch in what is know as apocalyptic imagery drawn from the Old Testament as well as from literature composed during the intertestamental period. Much of that imagery centers in sudden divine intervention, which results in terrible cosmos upheaval and judgment (Cf. Isaiah 13:10–13; Joel 2:1–2, 30–31).

The words of Jesus regarding the Temple were quite literally fulfilled in the fall and destruction of Jerusalem by Roman armies. This occurred in A.D. 70 after several years of Jewish insurrection. Nonbiblical historians relate that well over a million of Jerusalem's inhabitants were killed or removed from the city as captives. The magnificent Temple lay in ruins. We are told elsewhere that before the fall, the Christian community was warned, recalled the words of Jesus and fled the city.

The events are marked by trying times of persecution. False messiahs and false prophets will appear prior to the Lord's return and attempt to deceive the followers and disciples of Jesus. The New Testament clearly teaches that the Lord will return suddenly, unannounced and at a day and hour totally unknown to any human being. The Lord who promises to return also promises to be with his people in any age.

Watch and Pray 21:25–37

In light of the dire predictions of things to come, it is not surprising that Jesus earnestly warns his disciples to watch and pray. There will be signs pointing to heaven from which the Son of Man will come in power and glory. But people can grow weary of waiting and watching. Lest that great Day of the Lord come as a snare, God's people must watch and pray "in every time" so that we may escape judgment and stand before the Lord. As Jesus continues to teach each day in the Temple, he knows that the days are growing short. His great passion is soon to be upon him.

Passover and Passion 22:1–23:56

Jerusalem boasted its greatest population at Passover time. Two significant feasts were fused into one. Passover, commemorating the deliverance of their forefathers from slavery in Egypt, was observed 15 Nisan

(the evening of 14 Nisan; the Jewish day began at 6:00 P.M.), corresponding to our April. Unleavened Bread was celebrated for a week
following (Exodus 12; Leviticus 23:5–6). The city was so crowded
with pilgrims that the Roman procurator regularly brought reinforce-
ments from Caesarea to maintain order and quickly quell any rioting.
The spark of revolt, ever latent, could be mightily fanned by a festival,
which reminded Jews of a former deliverance form a foreign and hated
power. So it is on one of the chief festivals of the Jewish year that the
leaders search for a cause. They want to be rid of Jesus without foment-
ing the kind of tumult, which would occasion a serious uprising. They
find the means they were seeking in one of the twelve, Judas from the
village of Iscaroth, whom Luke describes as a traitor (6:16). For a fee
he is willing to betray the Lord.

Unleavened Bread and Passover 22:1–30

Jesus had made plans for the Passover meal. Peter and John now carry
them out. In an upper room assigned for their use, the two apostles
make all necessary preparations for food, unleavened bread and wine.
These were consumed in an elaborate ritual designed to retell and re-
live the experience of deliverance from bondage. To celebrate Passover
in Jerusalem was itself a special, much sought privilege. As Jesus assumes the position of host and father of the family, he announces once
again the nearness of his intensive suffering known as his passion.

During the meal, he institutes a sacramental action, which his church
observes in solemn but joyous remembrance of his death. The bread is
given to the disciples as his body. One of the cups of wine is proffered
as his blood of a new testament or covenant (Cf. Exodus 24:3–8). This
sacred act is a pledge of the forgiveness and reconciliation to which the
whole Old Testament sacrificial system typically pointed.

John and Peter prepare the meal. Judas, though seeing and hearing how
the ancient ritual is reinterpreted to proclaim redemption, has already
been snared by Satan. All the apostles are caught up in strife regarding position, priority and privilege in the kingdom. It was not the first
time such thoughts both dominated and beclouded their understanding of the kingdom of God (9:46–48). Jesus, the great Servant of God
(Isaiah 53), again reminds them that in his kingdom the key emphasis
must ever turn on emulating his own example. Those who faithfully

serve the Savior will reign with the Savior, assurance he provides as he symbolically refers to Israel and its twelve tribes.

Denial and Betrayal 22:31–62

Satan is busy. He entered Judas who became a willing instrument of treachery and betrayal. He desired the other apostles (Greek: you is plural in verse 31) in order to sift them like wheat. Jesus tells Simon Peter, who shamefully denies the Lord in spite of clear warnings, that his faith will not be permanently lost. It must be noted that Peter (and John) did enter the courtyard of the house of the High Priest. Whether they did so out of courage, curiosity or over-confidence, we do not know. In the hour of severe temptation, Peter fails. It was a test, which Peter, in his own strength, was simply not equipped to handle. Satan can be extremely subtle. He touches us at our most vulnerable point. Jesus realized that as he wrestled with Satan at the beginning of his ministry (4:1–13). Yet all is not lost. God can always bring good out of evil. Peter is restored by a most compassionate Christ in order to strengthen his fellow apostles.

In one of the many gardens located on the Mount of Olives Jesus again struggles with the full implications of his mission and ministry. In concern for the disciples, all of whom forsake him, he bids them pray in the time of testing (11:4). Jesus is strengthened in his own prayer as he resigns himself to the good and gracious will of his Father in heaven. The passion of our Lord is real, not a shame performance. The passion is a divine drama of redemption. But Jesus is not merely playing a role, donning a mask, wrapping himself up in a part until the curtain comes down. The hour of darkness that lay before him is finally upon him. Judas the traitor greets him as a devoted and loyal disciple who would show reverence and respect for his teacher. The chief priests, elders and Temple police are there to seize him. Jesus will not invoke divine authority to massacre with the sword. Jesus had prayed that God's will be done. It is being done!

Trial and Condemnation 22:63–23:31

After a night of humiliation and mockery, Jesus is arraigned before the Sanhedrin. Composed of seventy scribes, rabbis, elders, Pharisees and Sadducees, it exercised supreme religious authority over every sphere of Jewish life. The ruling High Priest presided over its sessions. Trials before the Sanhedrin were governed by strict and fair rules. In the case of this trial, several of those rules were broken. A majority of two was normally required for condemnation. In Jesus' case, the verdict appears to be unanimous. The prosecution consists of two crucial questions: Are you God's Anointed (Messiah)? Are you the Son of God? Judging his answer to be in the affirmative, the Sanhedrin declares him guilty of blasphemy, a crime for which he deserves to be put to death.

Unable, under Roman law, to carry out their death sentence, the Sanhedrin delivers Jesus to Pilate. They realize that a charge of blasphemy would never hold up in Roman court. It was obviously a religious issue. The assembly astutely charges Jesus with crimes that will be considered by a Roman forum: sedition, rebellion and treason against the state. Pilate sees through their scheme. But he cannot risk offending the supreme council. Luke recounts the ploy Pilate uses to shift responsibility to Herod. The puppet prince has his moment of glory when he can mock and humiliate the Lord. The silence of Jesus probably angered him more than anything else. It was considered to be an affront to the vacuous ruler whose throne was secured by Roman favor and his household guard. Luke the historian is quick to pick up the political nuances involved in the transaction. The Galilean king and Roman governor, at odds over incidents interpreted by Herod to be an infringement on his power (13:1–5), once again became friends. It must be remembered that Archelaus, a brother of Herod Antipas, had been removed as ruler of Judea and replaced by a procurator (3:1–6). So relations between Judea and Galilee were never truly amicable.

Neither Pilate nor Herod judged Jesus guilty of sedition or treason. He is therefore declared innocent of a capital crime against the state. Pilate, faced once again with the problem from which he desired to escape, wants to release Jesus. Instead, he chooses the path of compromise. He will scourge the prisoner and dismiss him. But the chief priests, rulers and people present will not settle for compromise. When Pilate offers to set Jesus free as a gesture of Roman clemency customarily observed on the Jewish Passover, the crowd clamors for the murderer and real seditionist, Barabbas (whose first name some claim was Jesus). The people prevail, not Pilate or Roman justice. Pilate simply cannot risk having a delegation from the Sanhedrin appear before Caesar with a charge of malfeasance against him. Consequences for Pilate could be especially dire if the delegation claimed that the governor had set free an insurrectionist who challenged the authority and power of Caesar. So Pilate gives sentence that their demands be granted. He releases Barabbas. He reminds Jesus to be crucified in accordance with Roman law. Jesus is taken from the hall of judgment to the mound of crucifixion known as Golgotha (Calvary), the place of the skull.

The condemned were forced to carry their own cross, which was in the shape of a T. A soldier carried a placard inscribed with the crime for which the criminal was being crucified. In the case of Jesus, the placard was affixed to his cross. It read: INRI (Jesus of Nazareth, King of the Jews), a bit of irony with which Pilate expressed his contempt for the Sanhedrin. When Jesus stumbled under the weight of the cross a certain Simon from Cyrene in North Africa, possibly a Passover pilgrim, was picked to carry it behind Jesus. Luke alone records the words Jesus directed to the weeping women. They are another reference to the Day of Judgment awaiting Jerusalem (21:5–24). If the innocent Jesus must suffer, how much more dreadful will be the suffering and catastrophe to come upon guilty Jerusalem!

Death and Burial 23:32–56

In this segment of his narrative, Luke includes informative material, which is not found in the other Gospels. He informs us of the intercessory prayer Jesus offered in seeking forgiveness for those who are crucifying him (23:34). This has been designated by the church as the First Word from the cross. Additionally, Luke brings us the immediate and assuring response of Jesus to the penitent criminal, the promise known as the Second Word. He records the Seventh Word of prayer in which Jesus commends his spirit in death to his Father in heaven (23:46), a prayer of utmost confidence drawn from Psalm 31:5.

Luke uses the Greek word to identify the commander of a platoon of one hundred soldiers (23:47), a Roman and a Gentile who sympathetically witnesses the final throes of Jesus on the cross. His unexpected confession represents a welcome shaft of light piercing an otherwise dark episode marking the first Good Friday. Luke draws other noted contrasts as well. One of the two perpetrators of evil hanging on either side of Jesus keeps heaping blasphemous insults on the Lord. The other, on whom tradition has bestowed the name Dismas, acknowledges his own guilt and the Lord's innocence. The one criminal reechoes the query of the Sanhedrin (22:67) and the jibes of the rulers (23:35). The other prays for a place in Jesus' kingdom. At midday, when the sun should be at its most brilliant best, a deep foreboding darkness falls over the land for three hours.

The Temple, which played such a major role in our Lord's ministry, and which served him as a classroom the last days of his earthly life, is affected by the events transpiring on Calvary's hill. The veil, separating and hiding the presence of God as were from the world, is split asunder. In the crucifixion of his Son, God's presence and heart have been opened to all. The Sanhedrin had mercilessly condemned Jesus and turned him over to the Roman authorities. Josephus, who had not voted with the majority, exemplifies rare boldness and courage in requesting from Pilate the body for decent burial. The daughters of Jerusalem bewailed the fate of Jesus. Women who had followed and ministered to him (8:1–3) went to the tomb with him. Then they lovingly prepared the spices and linen with which to render the Lord what they thought would be their final service. The great Friday in all human history was drawing to its close. The Sabbath began at 6:00 P.M.. The Jewish world would be at rest. The Lord of the Sabbath would, from all appearances, be at rest in his tomb.

Summary

It had been an event-filled week in the Savior's life, a week in which the shouts and blessings of Palm Sunday surrender to the jeers and rejection of Good Friday. The church calls it Holy Week. Jesus entered Jerusalem in the name of the Lord. As God's own Anointed, his mission was destined to lead to the cross. In the name of the Lord he had faithfully fulfilled his ministry.

As the early church pondered the passion of Jesus, it came more and more to see in it a portrait of the suffering servant of God depicted in Isaiah 52–53. Surely on the cross we are able to se a man of sorrows who is acquainted with grief, stricken, smitten of God and afflicted, numbered with transgressors who made intercession for them. Luke, in continuing his report to Theophilus (Acts 1:1), records as some of the earliest Christian proclamation that the God of our fathers glorified his Child, delivered up to Pilate, but raised up by God (Acts 3:13–15). That holy Child is Jesus, the servant who was wounded for our transgressions and who dies for our sins. The meal which Jesus gave his church is a continuing reminder of the sacrifice of his body and blood for the sins of the world.

This section concludes with a reminder of the Sabbath. The Jewish Sabbath (Saturday: the seventh day of the week) was ordained to commemorate the completion of God's work of creation. The Sabbath that followed Good Friday and preceded Easter Sunday was, in a certain sense, a commemoration of the completion of another great work of God, the work of redemption. Yet, in a far more profound sense, Jesus' mission and ministry to seek and save the lost was not completed. That would come with his triumphal resurrection.

Discussion

1. The crucifixion and death of Jesus is a preaching of God's law on the awful reality of sin. It is a preaching of God's gospel on the wonderful reality of grace.

2. Compare Luke's account of the words of institution with the liturgical formula delivered by Paul to the church in Corinth (1 Corinthians 11:23–26).

3. What is the significance of the various titles accorded Jesus in this section of Luke's Gospel?

CHAPTER EIGHT

Ministry of the Risen One
Luke 24:1–53

Why Seek the Living One Among the Dead?

Each major prediction of the passion recorded by Luke asserts the res-urrection as well. Luke also appends the reaction of the twelve to the Lord's pronouncement. They did not understand. They were unable to grasp what Jesus was saying (18:31–34). That first day of the week when women came to the tomb they fully expected to find him there. They came to anoint his body. It was in the third day, to be sure. But they did not believe that he would be raised up from the dead.

All of the four Gospels bear unqualified witness to the empty tomb. Each brings details and a perspective, which enable us to see the whole story of the resurrection. Luke quite likely had a copy of the Gospel of Mark at hand as he carefully examined the sources available for his research. It is also likely that Luke filled in some of the gaps in his own narrative from Mark's account. If so, he must have wondered and questioned the abruptness with which Mark concludes his report of the truly epochal event of all human history. (This assumes that Mark originally ends at 16:8.) Luke provides additional material. The ac-count of the dialog of Jesus with the Emmaus disciples brings a rich-ness of detail, which we otherwise would not possess (24:36–49). And only Luke records the precise question directed to the women in the tomb: Why are you seeking the Living One among the dead?

In the Tomb 24:1–12

Jesus was interred in the tomb provided by Joseph. Tombs were usually carved out of rock and sealed with a huge stone. The women who had devotedly ministered to the Lord (8:1–3) are told the truly astound-ing and unexpected news: He is risen as he had said! They immedi-ately share the news with the apostles. The reaction of the eleven is noted by Dr. Luke in medical terminology. The report of the women is called inane babbling. The apostles still do not grasp the meaning of the words they had heard from the lips of their Lord: The Son of Man must be crucified and rise on the third day.

Luke reports that only Peter was curious – or bold – enough to check out their story. Idle tale or fact? That is the question on which the truth of the entire gospel hinges. Even after seeing the linen burial cloths, Peter can only wonder concerning the things that have happened.

In Emmaus 24:13–35

Easter afternoon two disciples, one named Cleopas, are on their way to Emmaus, a village located some seven miles to the west of Jerusalem. As they exchange thoughts on all that had transpired they are joined by the Risen Lord. Dr. Luke informs us that their eyes were being held, for which reason they did not recognize him. (Some suggest they were looking into the bright, afternoon sun and for that reason failed to note it was Jesus.) Their faces register deep sadness. They relate the events, their own high hopes and the witness of the women. Yet they are not minded to believe that Jesus had actually risen. Neither do they comprehend the witness of the Old Testament to Jesus' suffering and glorification. It is in the breaking of bread that their eyes are opened. They serve as witnesses to the undoubted fact: The Lord is risen indeed!

In Jerusalem 24:36–53

The gospel, the good news that the Anointed of God died and rose from the dead so that forgiveness of sins might be proclaimed in his name, is all comprehended in the greeting of Jesus: Peace! The cross is real, not a sham symbol of defeat deftly turned into a sign of victory by disillusioned disciples. Redemption is a fact! The resurrection is real, not a cleverly devised fable intended to delude followers of deluded disciples. Peace is real. Forgiveness and salvation are proclaimed to all nations and people of all time. The Living One sent the Holy Spirit from the Father upon his apostles and disciples who finally did understand and grasp the meaning of his words, his mission and his ministry.

Luke's account of the Ascension of our Lord bears the mark of unadorned, factual simplicity. Jesus blessed them and was parted from them. They worshipped him, returned with great joy to the city in which they had experienced such sadness and praised and blessed God for the gift of all gifts: A Savior who is Christ the Lord!

Summary

The Christian community determined early to remember and commemorate the resurrection and presence of the Risen Lord in their worship and liturgy. They set aside Sunday, the first day of the week, as the day of the Lord, in confessional contradiction to Saturday, the seventh day of the week observed as the Jewish Sabbath. Christians would gather on the Lord's day to worship with great joy, pray, partake of the sacred meal and bless God for the redemption completed in the life, death and resurrection of his Son. A letter written to Emperor Trajan early in the second century refers to Christians who on an appointed day met before daybreak to recite a hymn (perhaps a Psalm) antiphonally to Christ and to bind themselves by a sacrament (Latin: sacramentum) by which they most likely referred to the Holy Communion. As late as A.D. 321, Emperor Constantine, who gave legal status to the Christian religion, spoke of "the venerable day of the Sun" and how it ought to be observed.

Following the outpouring of the Holy Spirit on Pentecost, narrated by Luke in Acts, commonly considered to be a sequel to the third Gospel, the apostles and disciples, clothed with power from on high, launched their dynamic witness to the ministry of their Lord. After his resurrection, Jesus himself set the tone for such witness. He rose the third day as he had promised, made his disciples certain of the reality of his resurrection, assured them of peace, commissioned them to proclaim repentance and forgiveness of sins in his name and blessed them as he took leave of them. They were indeed his witnesses. He had chosen them to proclaim all that he had said and done to seek and save the lost.

Discussion

1. Does Luke declare that Jesus is risen from the dead, or does he merely bear witness to the empty tomb?
2. Do the Emmaus disciples have counterparts in our contemporary world?

3. Why is the resurrection so foundational to the Christian faith? Who were the first witnesses of the resurrection? How did they react to the resurrection of their Lord?

Conclusion

The Lord's ministry of tragedy and triumph was played out over and against the background of growing opposition. After being hailed as the King who comes in the name of the Lord, Jesus is repeatedly confronted with the angry demand to show his credentials. What is his authority to challenge their authority? The religious officials quickly realize that they must be rid of him. Yet they are astute enough to recognize his immense popularity. Subtle means must be sought to discredit him. Even more subtle means must be found in order to charge him before both Jewish and Roman tribunals. Furthermore, the charges must stick. Blasphemy, insurrection and treason are such charges. Their nefarious plan is abetted by a greedy disciple willing to betray Jesus. The leaders will seize Jesus at the high festival. Jesus speaks solemnly of the disastrous consequences of their blind, misguided hatred as he pictures the utter destruction of both Jerusalem and its Temple.

While eating the ancient Passover meal with the apostles, Jesus institutes a new covenant. It is sealed with his own self-sacrifice. After hearing an arraignment before the Jewish Sanhedrin, Galilean king and Roman court, Jesus is summarily condemned to death, even though his guilt was never successfully proved. On the cross he continues to execute his ministry. Not only does he die as the suffering Servant of God; he prays for those who are responsible for the cruel deed, promises paradise to a penitent brigand who is suffering crucifixion with him and commends his spirit in complete trust to his Father in heaven.

Death could not hold him. True to his own predictions of his passion and resurrection on the third day, he comes forth from the tomb in triumphant victory over sin, Satan and death. Assuring the apostles of peace, he commissions them to proclaim peace to the world. They are to witness and declare repentance and forgiveness of sins in his name.

As the apostles fanned out to fulfill their ministry, they continued the ministry of Jesus. They proclaimed salvation and life in his name (4:12). That is the ministry of the church today: We are his witnesses.

Resources

Chapter One

1. He became man, conceived and born without sin, of the Holy Spirit and the Virgin, that he might become Lord over sin (LC II, 31).

2. The Holy Spirit makes me holy. How? The Holy Spirit reveals and preaches the word and kindles hearts to cling to it (LC II, 41).

3. The devil baits and badgers us on all sides, especially where conscience and spiritual matters are at stake (LC II, 104).

Chapter Two

1. The world is full of sects and false teachers, all of who wear the holy name as a cloak and warrant for their devilish doctrine (LC III, 47).

2. What is the kingdom of God? God sent his Son, Christ our Lord, into the world to redeem and deliver us from the power of the devil and to bring us life and salvation (LC III, 51).

3. The Son of God has become my Lord. He has redeemed me from sin, death and from all evil (LC II, 27).

Chapter Three

1. The devil baits and badgers us on all sides. His purpose is to tear us away from faith into unbelief (LC III, 104).

2. I pray for forgiveness because you have given the promise and set your seal to it, making it certain (LC III, 97).

3. We daily obtain full forgiveness through the word and through signs (sacraments) appointed to comfort and revive us (LC II, 55).

Chapter Four

1. There was no help until this only and eternal Son of God had mercy on our misery (LC II, 29).

2. We Christians should occupy ourselves daily with the word of God and carry it in our hearts and on our lips (LC I, 89).

3. The Holy Spirit carries on his work unceasingly (LC II, 61).

Chapter 5

1. We have heard what we are to do and believe. Now we learn how we are to pray (LC III, 1).

2. Where the word of God is proclaimed, there the blessed holy cross will follow. Let nobody think he will have peace (LC III, 65).

3. As we sin greatly against God, and yet he forgives through grace, we must always forgive our neighbor who does us harm (LC III, 94).

Chapter Six

1. To have a god is nothing else than to trust and believe him with your whole heart. Faith and trust alone make both God and an idol (LC I, 2).

2. Many a person things he has everything he needs when he has money and property. Such a man has a god, Mammon by name (LC I, 5–6).

3. God's kingdom comes to us in two ways: first, through the word and faith; secondly, through the return of Christ (LC III, 53).

Chapter Seven

1. The Lord's Supper was instituted by Christ without man's counsel or deliberation (LC V, 4).

2. Here we shall take our stand and see who dares to instruct Christ and alter what he has spoken (LC V, 13).

3. We go to the Sacrament because we receive there a great treasure, in which we obtain forgiveness of sins (LC V, 22).

Chapter Eight

1. He did none of these things for himself, nor had he any need of

them. Afterward he rose from the dead, swallowed up death and ascended into heaven (LC II, 31).

2. The proper place to explain all this: sermons throughout the year dealing at length with the birth, passion, resurrection and ascension of Christ (LC II, 33).

3. To be saved is nothing else than to be delivered form sin, death and the devil and to enter into the kingdom of Christ and live with him forever (LC IV, 25).

www.ingramcontent.com/pod-product-compliance
Lightning Source LLC
Chambersburg PA
CBHW031250090426
42742CB00007B/393